Failure

For my wife, Gabika
– A.A.

For my parents, Gad and Elia Alexander,
and for my family, on both sides of the ocean
– N.A.

Failure

Arjun Appadurai
and
Neta Alexander

polity

First published in 2020 by Polity Press

Polity Press
65 Bridge Street
Cambridge CB2 1UR, UK

Polity Press
101 Station Landing
Suite 300
Medford, MA 02155, USA

ISBN-13: 978-1-5095-0471-8
ISBN-13: 978-1-5095-0472-5 (pb)

A catalogue record for this book is available from the British Library.

Typeset in 11 on 14 pt Sabon by
Servis Filmsetting Ltd, Stockport, Cheshire
Printed and bound in Great Britain by CPI Group (UK) Ltd, Croydon

For further information on Polity, visit our website: politybooks.com

Contents

Acknowledgments   vi

Introduction: The Difference that Doesn't Make a
  Difference   1
1 The Promise Machine: Between "Techno-
   failure" and Market Failure   20
2 Creative Destruction and the New Socialities   46
3 Failure, Forgotten: On Buffering, Latency, and
   the Monetization of Waiting   70
4 Too Big to Fail: Banks, Derivatives, and
   Market Collapse   95
Conclusion: Failure, Remembered   118

References   126
Index   139

Acknowledgments

For helping me to prepare this book, I have to give special thanks to the PhD students in my two seminars on "Failure" in the Department of Media, Culture, and Communication at New York University. I am also grateful to the authors who contributed to the special issue on "Failure" of the journal *Social Research*, as well as to its editor, Arien Mack, for enriching my thoughts on this topic. My co-author, Neta Alexander, brought her acute intellect and expert knowledge to bear on every page of this book and made this collaboration a real pleasure. Finally, I am deeply grateful to my wife, Gabika, and our son, Kabir, who have taught me a great deal about the most important failures and successes in life.

Arjun Appadurai

First and foremost, I wish to thank New York University's intellectual community, which has nourished and sus-

Acknowledgments

tained me for many years and made this book possible. I am especially indebted to Anna McCarthy, Nicole Starosielski, and Faye Ginsburg for their ongoing support and for the numerous conversations that proved crucial for the ideas in *Failure*. I also wish to thank the editors of *Cinema Journal*, who published an earlier version of my work on buffering. Working with a writer of such accomplishment as Arjun Appadurai has been a rare privilege. The support and rigor of both Arjun and Polity's John Thompson turned a challenging endeavor into a highly enjoyable journey, and I thank them both for believing in this project from the very first moment. I am also grateful for the insightful and generous critical response of three anonymous readers, whose reports made this manuscript substantially richer. Lastly, I could not have written this book without the incredible support of my family: my parents, Gad and Elia Alexander, and my brother, Uri Alexander. I dedicate this book to them and to my partner, Bradley H. Kerr, whose love, compassion, and intellect have never failed me.

Neta Alexander

Introduction: The Difference that Doesn't Make a Difference

Commoditizing Failure

Mortal creatures that we are, humans are lamentably destined to fail. Yet, failure has recently emerged from the world of ordinary language and become a subject of both celebration and scrutiny. This book is a critical exercise in understanding the discourse of failure in our times, but it does not aim to reduce the idea of failure to an artifact of language, culture, or history, or to a social construction in the usual sense. We believe that the sense of failure is real and that it produces disappointment, regret, remorse, and other costly effects on individuals and groups. Yet, failure is not a self-evident property or quality of projects, institutions, technologies, or lives. Rather, it is a product of judgments that reflect various arrangements of power, competence, and equity in different places and times. As such, failure produces and sustains cultural fantasies and regimes

Introduction

of expectations. By reading failure as a judgment, we reveal its relation to memory, storytelling, and capital. This book therefore sets out to ask which failures are being forgotten, and which failures enter the collective memory and reshape our understanding of the world.

If we accept provisionally the idea that failure is not an immanent feature of any human artifact (such as a project, a technology, an institution, or a career), but is in fact a judgment that something is a failure, we are led inevitably to ask what events produce these judgments (history), who is authorized to make them (power), what form they must take in order to appear legitimate and plausible (culture), and what tools and infrastructures mediate these failures or make them ubiquitous (technology). Together, these factors generate what we call a "regime of failure," in which a certain epistemology, political economy, and dominant technology come together to naturalize and limit potential judgments about failure.

Our aim in this book is thus to show how such judgment protocols produce regimes of failure. We are especially interested in the ways in which contemporary capitalism configures financial and technological systems into an interconnecting apparatus that produces and naturalizes failure and creates the pervasive sense that all successes are the result of technology and its virtues, and that all failure is the fault of the citizen, the investor, the user, the consumer. This ideology can be summed up in the proposition that technology is always effective, if only its users were not so fallible. It is a "solutionism" forever trying to solve technological limitations or malfunctions by investing more capital in designing new technologies (Morozov 2013). From

2

Introduction

this perspective, we argue that looking at failure in our digitized world offers a novel point of entry into an immanent critique of the growing dependency on digital networks and mobile technologies – and of the opaque infrastructures that sustain them. More specifically, this book describes how some forms of failure operate within North America's finance and tech worlds, which are metonymies as the bi-coastal worlds of Wall Street and Silicon Valley. By limiting our investigation of failure to these two cultures, we hope to reveal how they monetize both forgetfulness and ignorance. The following chapters will therefore map the similarities between digital technologies and the financial market, studying the so-called "gig economy" (chapter 2), the monetization of waiting and latency (chapter 3), and the rise of the derivative form (chapter 4).

These case studies build on what one of us previously termed failure studies (Alexander 2017). One of the challenges in any attempt to study failure is that the term itself is often used interchangeably with a garden variety of other terms, among which are "accident," "disaster," "breakdown," and even "trauma." Reviewing each of these categories is beyond the scope of this work. Instead, we wish to isolate four schools of thought that will help us think creatively about failure: science, business, queer studies, and infrastructure studies.

The first field is modern science, where failures (in experiments, calculations, replicability) are treated as vital and indispensable features of the progress of the field, with the most explicit formulation about failure being Karl Popper's famous ideas about conjecture and falsifiability as the key hallmarks of fruitful hypotheses in the exact sciences (Popper 1963). With its emphasis on empirical falsification, Popperian thought was crucial to the development of a theory of science based on refutability. An experiment is successful if it refutes a false hypothesis and forces scientists to come up with a new, and often better, explanation for the same phenomenon. Failure is thus an essential and to some extent desired outcome; without it, progress is unattainable. In Silicon Valley, this model of scientific progress has been expended to include a blind faith in technological innovation (as we shall see in chapter 2).

The second major contribution to the study of failure has been made by the field of business studies (bridging technology, entrepreneurship, and investment), in which failure is increasingly acknowledged as something to encourage, cultivate, expect, and examine, especially where technical and commercial innovations are concerned. Much of the business literature is littered with clichés about learning from failure. Searching the word "failure" on Amazon generates over 20,000 books that proudly feature the F-word in their title. These include entrepreneurial guides such as *Failing Forward: Turning Mistakes into Stepping Stones for Success* (Maxwell 2000), *The Ten Commandments for Business Failure* (Keough 2011), and *WTF?! (Willing to Fail): How Failure Can Be Your Key to Success* (Scudamore and Williams 2018). The explosion of similar how-to-fail-better guides attests to Silicon Valley's ethos of failure as key to success. This need to celebrate failure could be explained by looking at the failure rates of startup companies. A 2016 industry report by leading venture capital firm Horsley Bridge Partners (HBP), based on aggregate data of over 7,000 investments made between 1985 and 2014, concluded that "Around half of all investments (in VC-backed startups) returned less than the original investment" (Evans 2016). According to Benedict Evans, an author and partner at the venture capital firm Andreessen Horowitz, the HBP report revealed the extent to which failure is essential to the innovation economy and its dependency on "unicorns" or extremely successful bets: "We try to create companies, products and ideas, and sometimes they work, and sometimes they change the world. And so, we see, in our world around half such attempts fail completely, and 5% or so go to the moon" (Evans 2016). Despite these paeans to failure, the links between business failures and innovation often remain as obscure as they were to such pioneers of social science as Frank Knight, Joseph Schumpeter, and Max Weber, who were interested in risk, profit, and innovation.

More recently, there has been a series of interventions by economists, sociologists, and other social scientists seeking to tackle the new innovation economy exemplified by Silicon Valley. These interventions are all indebted in some way to the work of Schumpeter on innovation and creative destruction in the history of capitalism, discussed more fully in chapter 2. The insights that emerge from this recent body of work include the following. The first is that the processes of investment, speculation, and innovation in the new economy are characterized not so much by rational expectations but rather by "fictions" (Beckert 2016), which can be defined as characterizations of the economic future which have no basis in empirical fact and seek to make the future the source for profit-making decisions. The second insight is that the production of value in this new economy has become increasingly skewed toward downstream value (value produced by speculative financial interests, short-term profiteering, and the rapid sale of potentially profitable enterprises in initial public offerings, or IPOs) rather than on upstream value, which is based on genuine scientific or technological discoveries (Janeway 2012). The third insight is that mainstream neoclassical economics has lost sight of the dynamics of these new economies, in which value is produced by massive financialization, along with its disruption and volatility, and not by the logic of supply, demand, and equilibrium (Mazzucato 2016). Each of these insights, which collectively support the argument that financial markets require more – rather than less – state regulation and supervision, also cast light on the cult of failure which reigns in the new economy, especially in Silicon Valley.

In order to move beyond the oversimplistic division between success and failure, the third field we will build on is queer studies. In recent years, queer scholars like Sara Ahmed, Lauren Berlant, Jack Halberstam, and Ann Cvetkovich have been convincingly pushing against a cult of "toxic positivity" or "cruel optimism" (Ahmed 2010; Berlant 2011; Halberstam 2011; Cvetkovich 2012). These various projects all aim to uncover the ways in which the neoliberal "promise of happiness" (Ahmed 2010) paradoxically results in increased anxiety, moments of breakdown, and "wounded attachments" to capitalist structures of power (Brown 1995). To do so, they focus their attention on isolating moments of trauma and helplessness: depression, anxiety attacks, writer's block, unfinished projects, or unemployment. By forcefully resisting the "happiness directive" and its idea of the "good subject" (productive, dutiful, mostly heteronormative consumer), queer scholars call for a

Introduction

more nuanced understanding of experience outside the framework of neoliberal "success" and its binary relation to "failure." Asking "what kinds of reward can failure offer us?" Halberstam states that,

> Failure allows us to escape the punishing norms that discipline behavior and manage human development with the goal of delivering us from unruly childhoods to orderly and predictable adults. Failure preserves some of the wondrous anarchy of childhood and disturbs the supposedly clean boundaries between adults and children, winners and losers. And where failure certainly comes accompanied by a host of negative affects, such as disappointment, disillusionment, and despair, it also provides the opportunity to use these negative affects to poke holes in the toxic positivity of contemporary thinking. (2011, 3)

What these theories offer us is nothing less than new temporalities of failure that expand our understanding of *failure as repetition, rather than difference*. We apply these theories to a reading of failure as a repeated, daily occurrence. It is not a trauma – with its binary temporality of "before" and "after" – but an "affective economy" (Ahmed 2004). Despite its subversive potential, this economy of failure often induces enduring anxieties and suffering.

This call for resisting the failure/success binary could also be found in the fourth, and last, methodology we build on: infrastructure studies, and more specifically the growing literature on maintenance and repair (Star 1999; Graham and Thrift 2007; Russell and Vinsel 2018). In a recent pledge to study "the maintainers" instead of "the innovators," Andrew L. Russell and Lee Vinsel remind us that the historical study of

7

maintenance and repair could be traced back to such classic works as John G. Burke's "Bursting boilers and the Federal power" (1966) – which argued that the "boiler disasters" of the nineteenth century were the result of both poor design and lack of maintenance (Russell and Vinsel 2018, 4). In the era of planned obsolescence, however, the possibility to sustain a culture of care is being questioned since the thing cared for is strategically built as a black box that cannot be easily or inexpensively fixed by the user. Once infrastructures have come to depend on highly interacted electric and computational systems, the important distinction between breakdown and failure is constantly challenged: "it becomes increasingly difficult to define what the 'thing' is that is being maintained and repaired. Is it the thing itself, or the negotiated order that surrounds it, or some 'larger' entity?" (Graham and Thrift 2007, 4). In chapter 1, we will return to this question in order to rethink the relation between breakdown and failure. While electronic and mobile technologies are designed to fail in order to sustain the culture of upgrades and replacements, users who hope to fix their devices face either an exhausting and costly uphill battle or an unavoidable failure as "right-to-repair" legislation is combated by tech companies (Koebler 2017). As a result, the lifespan of ubiquitous technologies such as smartphones has shrunk: the average mobile phone in Western nations is thrown away after only 11 months of use (Graham and Thrift 2007, 19). This problem has only worsened in the past decade, as the prices of electronics dropped. As a result, "the yearly e-waste mountain is growing, reaching 44.7 million metric tonnes (Mt) in 2016" (Leahy 2017).

Introduction

The growing interest in maintenance and repair therefore dovetails with the recent literature on "waste,"
which is often used as a synonym for failure (Shabi
2002; Maxwell and Miller 2012). Alongside its dis-
astrous effect on the environment, the exponential
growth in electronic waste (or "e-waste") attests to the
failure of globalization and innovation-driven capitalism to provide a free, open market that can potentially
bring prosperity to all. In practice, most e-waste is
produced in the West and dumped "offshore" in the
Global South (Leahy 2017). While we are not studying the wide-reaching implications of the global waste
economy, it provides an important reminder of the idea
that "infrastructure minus maintenance equals disaster"
(Russell and Vinsel 2018, 17). When earlier models of
maintenance and repair are neglected or forgotten, the
possibility of repeated failures quickly arises.

Chapter Breakdown

Building on these four different approaches, we argue
that failure is a volatile and variable concept. As the
following chapters will make manifest, we encounter
moments of failure on a daily basis, whether it is mani-
fested as a moment of digital lag, such as buffering, or
as losing money in the financial markets. The logic and
effects of *habitual failure* will therefore stand at the
center of this book. To borrow from Gregory Bateson's
famous definition of "information" as a "difference
that makes a difference" (1972), habitual failure as
perpetuated by both Wall Street and Silicon Valley is
the difference that doesn't make a difference (Alexander
2019). It is that which changes nothing: the non-event

Introduction

or the rapidly dismissed encounter with the helplessness of users and consumers.

That is not to argue that Wall Street and Silicon Valley share an identical attitude toward failure. In practice, Silicon Valley thrives on the idea that failure is key to innovation and success (as we shall see in chapter 2), while Wall Street heavily penalizes individual bankers and traders who do not get a deal done profitably via "Up or Out" promoting practices and other management techniques. While most startups are destined to fail, major banks have been declared "too big to fail" following the Great Recession. The differences between Silicon Valley and Wall Street are well known. Silicon Valley relies on technological innovation, venture capital, and the high probability of failed startups. Wall Street relies on the volatility of financial markets, the large and growing pool of consumer and corporate debt that guarantees the growth of finance capital, and the legal and regulative protections that safeguard large financial institutions from failure. In a word, Silicon Valley monetizes technological innovation while Wall Street monetizes financial innovation (while these two logics support and sustain each other).

Without denying these differences, we opt to identify and isolate the similarities between these two worlds in order to argue that their monetization of failure has wide-reaching impact. We will examine these commonalities throughout this book, starting with a discussion of failure as an epistemology and an affective economy in chapter 1. These commonalities, we argue, are not coincidental: They are based on the fact that Silicon Valley and Wall Street are mutually dependent parts of a shared ecology. Silicon Valley cannot exist with-

Introduction

out large and highly liquid pools of capital that can be invested strategically and shifted rapidly. Wall Street relies on innovations in digital technology to speed up trades; to increase the volume of financial transactions; to protect proprietary financial information; and to improve financial tools, devices, and screens. Thus, the symbiosis between Wall Street and Silicon Valley can be seen as the major distinctive feature of contemporary digital capitalism.

By closely looking at the failed promises made by Wall Street and Silicon Valley, this book reveals the understudied processes by which failure has been recast as a strategic means of valorization. Failure, we argue, has become a commodity. This is achieved by building a machine of broken promises aimed at denying or dismissing the existence of failure whenever it is experienced by the 99 percent. We develop this argument in chapter 1, where we offer a new, triadic typology of promises and their function within the world of both finance and Big Tech. Building on this new typology, we analyze the promise of convenience and its crucial role in the digital economy.

Our first chapter also introduces a detailed theory of failure by reading it as an epistemology, affect, and political economy. First, we define "techno-failure" as a moment of epistemological break as it fails to produce new knowledge about the machine and, in turn, a new understanding of the world. Second, we read failure as what Ahmed calls an "affective economy" and connect this analysis to the strategic production of forgetfulness by Wall Street and Silicon Valley. Third, we argue that failure is inherent to the market logic of capitalism and its dependency on credit, debt, and derivatives.

Drawing on chapter 1 and on Schumpeter's seminal work, chapter 2 argues that failure has evolved in contemporary digitalized economies so that it has become intimately linked to innovation, growth, profitability, and an incessant effort to bring possible futures into the present by anticipating failure and pre-empting it in a real-time loop between designer and user. The most striking feature of the ideology and discourse of failure, especially in what many regard as Silicon Valley culture, is directly descended from Schumpeter and involves the valorization of failure, sometimes in the guise of "disruption," and most often as a space of learning, correction, experimentation, and risk-taking. But failure in the startup economy has a highly specific meaning: it is not the failure of the body, when the programmer slumps over her desk or the call-center operator falls asleep in front of her screen. It is failure in the highly specific environment of fast-forward technology, low-cost software, and outsize profits from successful buyouts and public offerings in the digital realm. There is also a direct line from this embrace of innovation and volatility in capitalism to the peculiar centrality of potential failure in the recent design technologies of the post-industrial West. Where technology is concerned, failure is not admired in itself, but is seen as the ever-present cost of technological change. Failure therefore converts the user of digital or financial products into a perennial tester, a reporter on failures, whose behaviors, choices, wishes, and needs are channeled into design, testing, and experience protocols.

Focusing on the proliferation of the "gig economy," chapter 2 argues that the world of apps (and the startup firms that generate them, as well as the venture capitalists who bet on them) is not primarily about the destruction of previous forms of technology, production, or labor, though they have undeniable effects in these areas. Rather, it is the direct disruption of prior forms of sociality in an attempt to replace them with others by promising to enhance efficiency, convenience – or both.

This analysis of the obsolescence of social structures will serve as a basis for a discussion of failure, breakdown, and memory in chapter 3. As we will demonstrate, it is surprisingly common to trivialize, ignore, or simply forget the numerous ways in which technology breaks, malfunctions, or frustrates its users. Of course, this "forgetfulness" in itself points to a broader discursive system of doxas surrounding technology and the role it plays in users' lives. It attests not to the failure of memory, but to the success of cultural fantasies and collective imaginaries of technological utopias. When, and to what end, do we tell ourselves stories of failure? And when are moments of failure being masked or recast as part of a story of infinite progress?

Chapter 3 addresses these questions by studying buffering and "false latency" as part of a long history of waiting, lag, and delay in technological systems. We will show how moments of waiting and failure are constantly being monetized while the "global digital divide" separating different regions, generations, and classes is often denied (Ginsburg 2008; Mattern 2019). Bearing these various divides in mind, we argue that waiting is the key link between the two worlds this book studies: Waiting for credit approvals, waiting for the gap between receiving loans and paying interest on them, waiting for the reloading to be complete, waiting for the interruption to be resolved, waiting for the black box to restore itself so as to disappear from our attention. Waiting and queuing are widely known to be conditions of subordination, inequality, and discipline in societies throughout the world as they create "temporal inequalities" (Tawil-Souri 2017). So also with Wall Street and Silicon Valley, we are trained to wait as viewers and debtors, often in states of anxiety and anger, for the next moment of gratification, and we are also trained to forgive and forget the endless recurrence of traumatic buffering periods. This might explain the recent interest in the history and regimes of waiting (Tawil-Souri, 2017; Farman 2018; Janeja and Bandak 2018). Drawing on these studies, this chapter maps the paradox by which waiting is crucial for supporting business models that hail speed and instant gratification.

The world of Silicon Valley is the world of digital design, mega-apps, big data mining, and interface designs for new digital conveniences that both drive and exploit patterns in very large data sets (Appadurai 2019), while Wall Street is the world of investment banks, hedge funds, derivatives traders, financial analysts, and leveraged capital. Chapter 4 will therefore move the discussion from Silicon Valley to Wall Street by focusing on the Great Recession and the logic of derivatives. The bedrock of today's Wall Street lies in different forms of derivatives (all of which deal with the uncertain future value of commodities and companies) and such older forms as stocks, which aim to build markets on actual corporate performance, measured by such indices as profit–earnings ratio. The former now outweighs the latter by several orders of magnitude. Both Silicon Valley and Wall Street exploit the relation between risk, uncertainty, and profit (the keywords of

Introduction

Frank Knight's classic 1921 book, *Risk, Uncertainty and Profit*), but the bedrock of Silicon Valley is a new form of sociality (crystallized in the explosive growth in the value of apps studied in chapter 2), whereas the bedrock of Wall Street is consumer debt, which is then used to leverage high-end profits for financial elites through the mechanisms of arbitrage, leveraging, and volatility modeling. Both coastal cultures believe in outsize rewards, in which losses or failures are passed on to the consumer or end user, and mega-profits are streamed upwards to banks, hedge funds, and wealth managers. Venture capitalists are the most important players in Silicon Valley, and they are a specialized species of investor, with a special interest in technology as the focus of their speculative investments. Wall Street, on the other hand, is generally oriented to making profit from the volatility of financial markets; the debt dependence of customers, countries, and corporations; and the invention of new "derivative" forms for taking risks on other risks. Both breeds of investors (in Silicon Valley and on Wall Street) share the understanding that risk begets profit, that profit requires ceaseless innovation, and that failure can be passed downstream to the small debtor or innovator. Yet, Wall Street also knows that risk-taking requires an openness to failure, and hence both its generals and its troops have discovered myriad ways to shift the burden of failure to ordinary citizens, while holding on to outsize, even if occasional, profits.

Understanding Habitual Failure

Studying the flow of capital alongside the flow of information will help us build a theory of habitual

Introduction

failure. This will be achieved by exploring strategic
and inherent failure in such contexts as debt, crisis,
latency, and (dis)connectivity. We push against the
notion of "seamless" information and financial flows
and the language of immateriality, often used to disguise
their energy-consuming and environmentally destructive infrastructures. Both derivative instruments and
information storage (e.g. cloud computing) are scarce
resources marketed as infinite by promoting the idea
that scarcity can and should be eliminated in the age
of seamless connectivity. Theirs is a failed promise of
infinite progress, an unattainable utopia that serves to
deny the devastating environmental, psychological, and
social price needed to sustain these systems of power.

For the experience of failure to be fully turned into
a driver of digital capitalism, it requires a method for
forgetting failure, so as to allow its continuous repetition. The customer or end user must be trained to deny,
occlude, or forget failure so that she can be receptive to
the next failure. This is accomplished in the current era
of digital risk-taking and choice-making by the way in
which failure is re-framed as an illusion, a form of electronic noise, or as a sign of incompetence on the part of
the user (Goffman 1974). In the case of financial products, which encourage ordinary citizens to both take
extraordinary risks and be endless producers of the debt
that fuels highly exploitative and extractive financial
practices (see chapter 4), the initial framing takes risk
to be a natural and unavoidable feature of the world of
money and finance, though it is in fact a relatively recent
artifact of history and policy (Beck 1986). The second
piece of the frame is to imagine and project citizens as
wise and prudent only when they put their savings into

abstract, risky, and long-term assets (such as mortgages, insurance policies, and pension funds). The third part of this framing encourages consumers to become active players in stocks, bonds, options, futures, and other specialized financial instruments, gradually encouraging them to equate prudence with risk-taking. The last piece of the framing teaches customers that it is wise to leave their risk-taking decisions in the hands of professionals and experts (counselors, brokers, traders). When failures occur (shrinking pension assets, inadequate insurance coverage, collapsing mortgages, falling housing values, unrepayable loans), the customer is taught to re-frame these failures as inevitable products of her naiveté or lack of understanding, her incompetence in choosing the right product, and her inability to properly understand both her own level of risk tolerance and the inherent volatility of financial markets. Based on this re-framing, which is conveyed through numerous channels, from banks and hedge funds to online seminars and business news coverage on TV and newspapers, the customer is quickly brought back into the cycle of debt, risk, and (very likely) repeated financial loss.

This is how framing and re-framing work to ensure that ordinary citizens and customers continue to take risks they cannot afford and do not understand, and that they increasingly take on debt that lubricates the operations of the financial industry without recognizing that their role is to fail, and then to fail again.

In a similar manner, digital media fail all the time, but they do so within a discourse hailing their magical, quasi-religious, qualities (Chun 2008). As chapter 3 demonstrates, "techno-failure" is a twofold process: first a machine breaks or malfunctions, and then a user might (or might not) identify a failure. These ubiquitous failures, however, are often denied. This denial takes place when the idea the technical failure might reveal is instantaneously replaced with another, less threatening idea. In the case of buffering, for example, the unpredictable moment of delay and suspended time might be attached to reassuring ideas like "I forgot to reconnect the router" or "this temporary disturbance will soon end." What remains concealed is the idea that buffering induces a "perpetual anxiety," which, in turn, reveals a structure of meaning to our world: the fact that we increasingly rely on machines and infrastructures whose logic is invisible to most users (Alexander 2017). Re-framing buffering as a technical, soon-to-disappear nuisance involves the very same system of denial we could find in Wall Street whenever a financial downturn occurs.

Thus, the infrastructural amnesia on which the financial and digital industries rely, such that failures are forgotten fast enough so that new failures can be accepted, is based on the constant framing and re-framing of the experience of loss, exploitation, dissatisfaction, and frustration that does not prevent repeat engagement with the medium or instrument which is the source of the failure. To return to our definition of habitual failure, no difference is being made. It still might hurt, yet the pain is being displaced and denied in a way that prevents structural, political changes.

In this cycle of denial and displacement, only one thing is certain, the certainty of failure as repetition and the repetition of failure. Here we anticipate our concluding argument, which will be more fully elaborated at the end of this book. If, as we argue, habitual failure

Introduction

doesn't make a difference, how can we isolate, identify, and mitigate its potentially destructive effect on our lives? In short, how can we better remember the failures of the (recent) past, and resist the monetization of those that are yet to come?

Chapter 1
The Promise Machine: Between "Techno-failure" and Market Failure

Introduction

After defining failure as a judgment in our Introduction, we argued that many repetitive and daily failures are being quickly dismissed or forgotten. To start unpacking the conditions by which failure is being either acknowledged or denied, this chapter will introduce the concept of "techno-failure" – the breakdown or malfunction of technological tools such as mobile devices, digital interfaces and infrastructures, or personal computers.

Before we can approach case studies of technological and financial failures such as buffering or the derivative form (which will be explored in the second half of this book), we must first familiarize ourselves with a broader theory of failure. This will be achieved by studying failure as epistemology, affect, and political economy. In Silicon Valley and Wall Street, failure is not an accidental, unexpected one-time event; it functions, rather, as a commodity and as such it is being monetized, exchanged, and valorized. But how exactly does failure gain value? By producing and sustaining a machine of broken promises. Both finance and tech share an underlying adherence to a new taxonomy of promises: "the Austinian promise," "the agonistic promise," and "the delayed promise" – all of which will be defined and explored throughout this book.

Finally, we tie this triadic categorization to the prominent promise of convenience, with its emphasis on immediacy and instant gratification. Building on the work of Thomas Tierney (1993), we read convenience as much more than the utilitarian desire to maximize pleasure and avoid pain; it signals, instead, a paradigm shift in our relation to our bodies and lived environments. Paradoxically, the pursuit of convenience – a broken promise perpetuated by Silicon Valley and Wall Street alike – has led to the rise of anxiety, debt, and crisis on an individual and collective scale.

The Denial of Failure

While failure is everywhere, it is not always recognized as such. Some banks are "too big to fail," while the internet is often described as immune to failure thanks to its decentralized and supposedly immaterial nature. In practice, however, this perceived invulnerability is very far from characterizing a complex, global network based on cloud architecture and underwater fiber-optic cables. Providing an alarming account of the growing dependency on cloud computing, Tung-Hui Hu warns that "A multi-billion-dollar industry that claims 99.999 percent reliability breaks far more often than you'd think, because it sits on top of a few brittle fibers the width of a few hairs" (2016, ix). As Hu points out, the tendency to revert to abstraction when it comes to digital infrastructures is not only misleading – it also holds enduring political and philosophical implications. The discourse of "immateriality" (which will be further discussed in chapter 3) is a crucial tactic to sustain the power of the economic and digital divides and to present the internet as an obscure, infinite, and ahistorical system of connectivity and access to information. One of the reasons digital immateriality is such a prominent myth is that it helps users forget the physical, ever-expanding, global infrastructure that makes surfing the web feasible. As media and infrastructure scholars repeatedly stress, it is crucial to explore the material conditions on which the internet is based (Thackara 2005; Parks and Starosielski 2015).

To understand why and how this fragility is so often denied, we must first develop a theory of "techno-failure." This is different from simply mapping a series of technological fiascos or failed products, as these are often studied within the familiar pattern of "failure as success." To that extent, a failed invention such as the 1929 "cat phone" proved crucial for the advent of cochlear implants, and the failed 50mm film paved the way for the CinemaScope screening format (Belton 2009; Sterne 2009). Pushing against this prominent pattern, Lisa Nakamura reminds us that "characterizing an object as a failure is a much more successful strategy if it was an early iteration of one that later became extremely popular or admired" (2009, 87). Instead, she focuses her attention on a more ubiquitous form of failure: the PowerPoint presentation. As anyone who has ever attended an academic conference knows all too well, our attachment to the visual memory aide of the slideshow often results in nerve-wracking moments of suspense, helplessness, and heartfelt cries to the never-on-site technical support. In Nakamura's words, "Moments of presentational failure lard conferences and classrooms like raisins in a pudding – they are everywhere, albeit not all the time" (2009, 87). Drawing our attention to vernacular failure – rather than to epic commercial failures like Apple's Lisa computer – can help us start unpacking the process by which some failures enter the collective memory and imagination while others are simply ignored.

Yet, Nakamura's attentiveness to the ubiquity of techno-failure does not absolve her from the tendency to focus on the user – and not on the inherently precarious machines and infrastructures. She half-jokingly concludes her PowerPoint obloquy with the following pledge: "Rather than bemoaning our ability to correctly manage the necessary welter of cords, adapters, remotes, power sources, and flash drives, perhaps we ought to learn to view these supposed failures as marks of distinction and paradoxical displays of expertise" (2009, 87). Are we to become experts in failing? Is the solution truly "to fail better," as both Samuel Beckett (1995) and Mark Zuckerberg urge us to do? This chapter aims to answer these questions by recasting failure as a commodity. Technological failures such as limited battery life, digital lags, or frozen, irresponsive screens effectively support a business model of upgrading and planned obsolescence that is crucial for the proliferation of "habitual new media" (Chun 2016). Within the culture of beta testing, maintenance and repair are no longer desired. In practice, tech behemoths like Apple render them all but impossible. Unlike a decades-old boiler, an iPhone is strategically designed as an opaque and proprietary tool that can only be repaired in designated Apple Stores. In 2018, Apple lobbied against legislation that would make it easier for iPhone users to repair their smartphone and other electronics (Koebler 2017). The legal battle against the "right-to-repair" legislation introduced in the state of California exposed the lengths to which tech giants like Apple, Microsoft, and Samsung are willing to go in order to prevent both customers and independent electronic shops from prolonging the lifespan of their devices (Koebler 2017).

While planned obsolescence is crucial for the ongoing success of the gadget industry, in the sphere of stocks and derivatives, failure can quickly turn into profit by "short selling" (e.g. buying a stock and waiting for its price to decline). When it comes to tech, problems such as slowness, disconnection, or unrepairable hardware can be strategically implemented to force users to opt for "premium services." These supposed failures are therefore successful attempts in building a market desperate for new models and "disruptions" (Silicon Valley's favorite keyword). Writing about how transmission technologies create "a new class system," Sean Cubitt contends that "the purpose of control over information is to delay transmission. We think we pay more for premium service delivery of news and entertainments; in fact, the money pays for timely arrival, and its absence ensures a deliberately delayed and often downgraded delivery" (2014, 4). As a result, there exists a digital divide that further individualizes users' media experiences.

Yet techno-failures still seem to function as "raisins

in a pudding," to use Nakamura's metaphor. With its emphasis on ubiquitous failure, her essay joins a growing body of literature reviewed in our Introduction. Building on the four schools of thought we previously surveyed – science, business literature, queer studies, and infrastructure studies – we wish to isolate three categories that will prove particularly productive for our argument regarding the centrality and strategic use of failure in Wall Street and Silicon Valley: First, techno-failure as essential to the production of new knowledge about the machine and, in turn, a new understanding of the world; second, failure as what Sara Ahmed calls an "affective economy"; and third, failure as inherent to the market logic of capitalism and its dependency on credit, debt, and derivatives. These categories respectively explore the *epistemology*, *affect*, and *political economy* of failure.

The Epistemology of Techno-failure

While Karl Popper offers us a set of principles that can serve to distinguish a failed scientific theory from a successful one, it is Martin Heidegger who can be seen as the godfather of the growing discipline of Failure Studies. In Heideggerian thought, the world is "present-at-hand" – it is revealed to us by way of different practices and encounters with tools or objects. Yet, the relational function of objects – the way they produce different substances and function within a given environment – only becomes visible once they fail, in the moment in which "the tool suddenly demands attention to itself" (Graham and Thrift 2007, 8). There exists, however, an important distinction between failure and breakdown.

Heidegger's *vorhanden* ("objectively present" in the newer translation, or "present-at-hand" in the older) focuses on moments of breakdown. While failure occurs from the standpoint of a goal in the world, breakdown might happen without our direct involvement. Take, for example, the following description of a frequent computational failure:

> Someone sits at a word processor focused on the text at hand and all of a sudden the computer freezes. The trustworthy world that developed around the computer – the open book, the keyboard, the screen, the cup of coffee; in short, the entire mutually referring network that Heidegger calls a world – is abruptly destroyed. The computer changes from being one of the handy or ready-to-hand that shape this world to what Heidegger calls something *vorhanden* ... Its transparency is transformed into opacity. The computer can no longer be utilized in the practice of writing, but abruptly demands interaction with itself. (Verbeek 2004, 79)

This moment, however, requires a more detailed attention. The Heideggerian attempt to bring together rupture and epistemology – the moment of failure and the production of knowledge – is put to the test in the age of digital and mobile technologies. When they break, these handheld devices do not necessarily germinate new knowledge on either their inner workings or the world in which they operate. While a tool such as a mirror or a glass-made cup might violently shatter into pieces (and therefore draw attention to its fragile materiality), a smartphone often breaks down quietly and opaquely, in the guise of a sudden moment of lag, a prolonged lack of response, or a "dead" battery.

As mentioned above, companies like Apple and Samsung have so far resisted any attempt to legalize the users' "right to repair." This rejection of maintenance and repair has far-reaching consequences: "For without that capacity (for repair) the world cannot go on, cannot become ready-to-hand again" (Graham and Thrift 2007, 3). Moreover, the important distinction between breakdown and failure is constantly challenged once we are forced to reconsider Heidegger's argument regarding the ability to easily differentiate humans and tools. As Timothy Barker recently argued, technology should now be read "as a process, rather than as an object" (2018, 10), and media scholars should therefore focus on "the production of the conditions for the possibility of experience" (2018, 7). If digital technology should be studied as a process or as an assemblage – and not as a series of isolated objects or interfaces – how can we determine when and why it fails, or which criterion of failure to apply? What kind of work is needed in order to isolate "the conditions for the possibility" of failure?

This scholarly pursuit is further complicated by the fact that our failed technologies do nothing more than further obstruct the underlying logic and hidden infrastructures that sustain them. This results in "the disappearance of technology," a problem addressed by Mark Jarzombek (2016) and others. In Jarzombek's words, "the word technology is now meaningless, the residue of an anthrocentric worldview of Man and Tool and the elusive promise of *techne*. Technology has morphed into a bio-chemo-techno-spiritual-corporate environment that feeds the Human its sense-of-self. We are at the beginning of a new history" (2016, 5). This paradigm shift transforms moments of breakdown into a chain of failures: the failure to trace and understand the source of the problem; the failure to repair the tool; and, as we shall see in chapter 3, the failure to remember the breakdown in order to challenge the prominent narratives surrounding digital technologies (such as their infinite seamlessness or supposed immateriality).

Put differently, there are two reasons why failure no longer functions as an epistemological apparatus: first, we can no longer separate tools, bodies, and environments; second, even when our technological tools break, they do not become transparent as their underlying logic and inner working remain hidden from the user. Due to the rising complexity of networks and algorithmic systems, the engineers or designers behind these devices often remain in the dark themselves, a notion that will only grow stronger in a world based on machine-learning algorithms and AI (O'Neil 2016). Worse still, there is an ever-growing division of labor: while underpaid workers mine coltan in the Congo or manufacture electronics in the Global South, highly paid experts who mostly reside in Western countries and the coastal cities in the United States are tasked with designing and engineering these devices (Mantz 2008). These strategic divisions of labor are used to create "Geeky Silos," described by Gillian Tett as "the idea that small cadres of technical experts, hidden from public view, are pushing the frontier of their particular disciplines in ways that could in fact be quite dangerous" (2010). One result of this expert culture is the ever-growing industry of call-center helplines tasked with helping users to deal with the "mass, routine failure in computer systems" (Graham and Thrift 2007,

12). Once again, the users are mostly located in the West while the workers assisting them are recruited in the Global South.

This lack of transparency is the *raison d'être* of the "Black Box Society" (Pasquale 2016). Algorithmic systems, including those used in finance, are hidden behind a smoke screen of intellectual property and specialized knowledge. In his analysis of this black-box model, Frank Pasquale asserts that "We cannot understand, or even investigate, a subject about which nothing is known. Amateur epistemologists have many names for this problem. 'Unknown unknowns,' 'black swans,' and 'deep secrets' are popular catchphrases for our many areas of social blankness" (2016, 1). This information asymmetry, he argues, has led to a growing interest the field of "agnotology," which studies the "structural production of ignorance, its diverse causes and conformations, whether brought about by neglect, forgetfulness, myopia, extinction, secrecy, or suppression" (2016, 1). Building on the work of Robert Proctor and Londa Schiebinger (2008), who made the term famous through discussing the politics of deliberately concealing or providing misleading information, Pasquale contends that the failure to understand our machines is far from accidental. It is manufactured and sustained by tech and finance conglomerates in order to prevent the kind of shared knowledge and education needed for political resistance.

This epistemological rupture in the user's ability to learn from failure is further complicated by the neoliberal co-option of techno-failure. As we shall see in chapter 2, failure and testing have become prominent features of post-industrial design and its future-oriented temporality. Technological design's modern project was trying to avoid failure, but the post-industrial logic is that of "fail early, fail often" (Tonkinwise 2016). Techno-failure is therefore a repeated, daily occurrence rather than a one-time event. The numerous moments in which a computer screen "freezes" – a moment that can easily make one skip a heartbeat – are in fact part of product testing, urging us to "send report" or "ignore" (a choice that more often than not results in ignoring and, in turn, forgetting).

This method is useful for the study of a specific sub-category of techno-failure: "planned obsolescence." It is a business model based on designing a product with an artificially limited lifespan: "the rationale behind this strategy is to generate long-term sales volume by reducing the time between repeat purchases" (Bao et al. 2010, 296). In the business literature, this is often described as "shortening the replacement cycle" (Bao et al. 2010). In his seminal 1960 book, *The Waste Makers*, Vance Packard argued that this harmful business model is a quintessentially American invention. Building on Packard's groundbreaking analysis of American consumerism, Giles Slade traces the early incarnation of this business model in the United States to 1913, when the introduction of the electric starter in automobiles "raised obsolescence to national prominence by rendering all previous cars obsolete" (2007, 11). This, however, was only the beginning of the endless attempts to produce "repetitive consumption" of the very same product. The "annual model change," whose most recent incarnation is the ceremonial launch of a new iPhone, was introduced in the 1920s by General Motors and other car manufacturers. The idea that the 1923

Chevrolet was somehow better than the 1922 model paved the way for what Slade calls "psychological, progressive, or dynamic obsolescence" (2007, 3). This alarming description begets troubling questions: How can we theorize failure in the age of obsolescence? If a technology was designed to fail, should its failure be seen as a success? And what can the failure of the once-dominant business model of maintenance and repair teach us about the underlying logic of neoliberalism?

Furthermore, the idea of obsolescence has not spared academia or the creative industries; it has expanded from commodities to human "knowledge workers" (Terranova 2000). The notion that academics, freelance writers, and other knowledge workers must "update" their skillset or else become obsolete will be discussed in chapter 2, which studies the obsolescence of social structures. For now, this brief discussion of obsolescence can help us foreground some of the ways in which failure is being co-opted or reinterpreted by conglomerates and the tech industry. The failure-by-design model paves the way for affective economies that are often ignored by both users and media scholars.

The Affective Economy of Failure

To start unpacking the uniqueness of failure in the entrepreneurial age, we must also consider failure as an "affective economy." Challenging the idea that emotions are "a private matter," Sara Ahmed suggests instead that we should think about them in terms of "affective economies": "rather than seeing emotions as psychological dispositions, we need to consider how they work, in concrete and particular ways, to mediate the relationship between the psychic and the social, and between the individual and the collective" (2004, 119). For Ahmed, affect works like capital due to its accumulation and circulation in the social sphere; like capital, it does not reside in any specific object, sign or commodity, but is *a movement between* different objects and signs. This psycho-economic model builds on the Freudian idea of repression as a process by which an emotion is perceived but its origin is left unconscious. As a result, "what is repressed from consciousness is not the feeling as such, but the idea to which the feeling may have been first (but provisionally) connected" (2004, 120). A fear of flight, for example, can still be perceived as fear. However, if we accept the Freudian depth model, we can argue that fear of flight was originally attached to the fear of death – not to the fear of airplanes. The feeling is now attached to a specific external stimulus (in this case, being up in the air) while concealing or denying its true cause and the horror it might evoke.

Building on Ahmed and complicating Heidegger's model, we wish to argue that failure functions as an affective economy when the idea it might reveal is instantaneously replaced with another, less threating idea. In chapter 3, we apply this argument to buffering and other unexpected digital lags, arguing that these moments of delay and suspended time might be attached to reassuring ideas like "this temporary disturbance will soon end." What remains concealed is the idea that buffering induces a "perpetual anxiety" due to its liminal sphere of activity and passivity, helplessness and control, and viewing *as* waiting (Alexander 2017). Recasting buffering as a technical, soon-to-disappear nuisance therefore involves the very same system of "difference and displacement" described by Ahmed. When it comes to digital culture, perpetual anxiety always lurks in the back of users' minds: whether it takes the form of "connectivity anxiety," "battery-life anxiety," or, with the emergence of "connected homes" and the Internet of Things (IoT), an entirely new set of anxieties "about the ways media devices might be looking back at us" (Petruska and Vanderhoef 2014, 33). In that sense, the affective economy that buffering might reveal is only one example of an anxiety caused by the combination of the need to wait for an unpredictable length of time and an excruciating feeling of helplessness when facing black boxes.

More generally, there are two main ideas that are being replaced and displaced when it comes to technological failure: First, that digital technology is neither magic nor an immaterial phenomenon. Its software, code, and algorithms operate according to a strict set of rules, while its hardware is subject to wear and tear, malfunction, and misuse. It is therefore precarious, unreliable, and strategically unrepairable. Second, that what was once thought of as a means to conquer nature has evolved into an extension of information capitalism. Computational technology is a system of power and control based on information asymmetry and the extraction of data and attention (which have come to replace more traditional models of value such as labor time).

Still, this is not how users usually register these ideas. From the user's perspective, similar thoughts might take the form of the anxious realization that she is no longer in control of her machine, that she does not know how to fix it, and that someone else is monetizing her uncertainty. Often, these anxieties are displaced from the machine to either the self or other humans. This can take the form of blaming others for the disruption ("the neighbors are stealing my bandwidth"), or accusing oneself for mishandling the router or wandering off the connectivity zone. Even when the slowness is strategic or systemic (which, as we will see in chapter 3, is very often the case), users rarely blame the technology, its designers, or the company manufacturing and marketing their personal devices and digital services.

These, however, are not private or subjective emotional and cognitive reactions. Studied as an affective economy, this displacement of ideas regarding our human–machine dependency can be seen as a form of a *collective (or collectivized) failure*. Still, this failure is often discriminatory: technological failures are more frequent and substantial when users lack the digital or algorithmic literacy needed to understand the design and infrastructure of their black boxes. This is especially problematic as digital technologies and services are becoming more dependent on highly complex algorithms. The dangers of these systems, which are beyond the scope of this book, have been the focus of numerous important works in the last decade (O'Neil 2016; Cheney-Lippold 2017). As John Cheney-Lippold (2017) argues, for example, one could be sent to prison, denied life-saving medical treatment, or targeted by a weaponized drone based on the calculation of opaque algorithms.

Recognizing the importance of this growing literature, we would like to focus our attention on more habitual and ubiquitous forms of techno-failure. As daily moments of disconnect and waiting tend to be sporadic and unexpected, users encounter them in different places and at different times. Their ability to fully understand these breakdowns and subsequently repair them – or at the very least hold tech companies accountable for the predatory business models that produce them – is extremely limited.

The Economy of Failure

Bringing together affect and capital, Ahmed is one of numerous scholars who have rigorously engaged with the idea that capitalism's "calculating attitude," as famously theorized by Max Weber, has been pushed to its extreme in the past few decades. As a result, the self is now widely regarded "as a kind of enterprise, seeking to enhance and capitalize on existence itself through calculated acts and investments" (Rose 1999, 164). Preventing a political or structural critique of neoliberalism, this cult of calculation gave birth to a world in which when we fail, as we so often do, we only have ourselves to blame.

As chapter 2 will demonstrate, we can trace the monetization of failure and its warm embrace by Silicon Valley to the mid-century discovery of innovation, risk, and even crisis by such thinkers as Joseph Schumpeter. As both Marx and Schumpeter made very clear, market failure is a normal part of the business cycle, and not only the endpoint of capitalism's overall movement. Failure is thus an inherent feature of capitalism; it is the rule rather than the exception. While Marx was among the first philosophers to (wishfully) argue that capitalism is doomed to fail, Schumpeter developed a more specific theory of the role failure plays in the expansion and flow of capital. Schumpeter, an Austrian-born political economist who lived and worked in the United States, agreed with Marx that capitalism would eventually collapse. However, unlike Marx's prediction of a proletarian revolution, Schumpeter believed that the conditions necessary for what he called "creative destruction" might gradually disappear. In his seminal *Capitalism, Socialism and Democracy*, originally published in 1942, Schumpeter argued that failure is inherent in capitalism's "business cycles" of prosperity and decline. He isolates two kinds of failures: The first is the failure of new innovations designed and manufactured by risk-taking entrepreneurs. In a process akin to natural selection, many of these products will fail – while paving the way for better technologies and the discovery of new markets. The second kind of failure is, paradoxically, what happens when a new innovation succeeds: as a result, the competitors fail (and so, to use a recent example, Netflix is often blamed for "killing" Blockbuster and other market leaders in the video rental industry). In both scenarios, failure is the engine of innovation and expansion, the two forces on which capitalism depends. More recently, this led to the rise of the risk-bearing entrepreneur, one of the most dominant figures of twenty-first-century neoliberalism and its *"homo economicus."*

The current failure of neoliberalism, however, is not only the failure to regulate monopolies such as Silicon Valley's tech giants. Building on Schumpeter, one of us has argued that the 2008 recession was in fact the epitome of a linguistic, rather than solely economic, failure (Appadurai 2015). The market collapse was not only a direct result of greed or lack of regulation, but also an inherent feature of the derivative economy. The derivative functions as a "promise about the uncertain future," and the failure of the derivatives market is a result of a set of systemic and risky failed promises. To push this further, we wish to argue that the problem is not necessarily the bet on an uncertain future – but that this bet is leveraged and made into debt, rather than into equity (see chapter 4).

This theory promotes our understanding of failure as a direct result of a machine of broken promises. This machine is the *raison d'être* of both Wall Street and Silicon Valley, and its unpacking requires a taxonomy of promises.

The Machine of Broken Promises

The idea of the promise is central to our analysis of failure. We wish to distinguish between three categories of promise: *Austinian*, *agonistic*, and *delayed*. As different as these might seem, they all function as performative utterances that create the conditions of their own truth. By making a promise, one creates a world in which such a promise might be fulfilled. Often, a promise is thought of as an option followed by a conclusion: it is based on an if/then statement or a conditional statement such as "if you finish your homework, then you will be allowed to eat ice cream." These kinds of promises mostly take place under conditions of certainty: there is nothing that might prevent the parent from buying and providing the ice cream, for example. The triadic structure of the promise that we are interested in, on the other hand, relates to uncertainty, risk, and contingency. These are promises that either are made to be broken or are very unlikely to be fulfilled. Their failures are thus intrinsic and predictable, and yet these performative acts still define the underlying logic of the financial markets and, to a lesser degree, the tech industry.

A. *Austinian/performative promise.* Named after J.L. Austin's (1975) work on performatives and their conditions of felicity, this general category of speech acts includes (among many others) any contract between two sides in which the losing party promises to pay the winning party an agreed-upon sum of money based on the future prices of various types of assets. Thus, the contract is *a promise about the uncertain future.* This kind of promise is performative to the extent that the very act of stating the promise has the effect of binding the two participants. The agreement and the promise are one and the same. More importantly, it is speculative as it takes into account probabilities and contingencies and therefore consists of a risk factor, because the price at the end of the stipulated period is unknown and unknowable. When one signs such a contract, one knows that one might lose money or assets.

B. *Agonistic promise.* Unlike the pure Austinian promise, an agonistic promise requires two parties whose promises to pay one another have to be simultaneous and mutually exclusive, so that both promises (which together compose the contract) meet the same conditions of felicity. The second key feature of this sort of agonistic promise is that it depends on the endless tradability of any particular bundle of assets (such bundles are often called securities), something that resembles the endless circulation of money. Failure – or collapse – occurs when the system-wide relations between the buyers and sellers of these assets enter into a crisis because there are no buyers for large amounts of these instruments, thus creating a monumental pile of debt without another buyer left to pick up the mountain of accumulated risk. This distinction – between too many sellers and very few remaining buyers – is crucial, as it will help us move the discussion from individual failure to collective failure. The agonistic promise underlying derivative trades, which will be studied in chapter 4, is an example of what legal theorists call "aleatory" contracts, contracts whose fulfillment depends on future conditions which are unknown to both contracting parties. Both aleatory contracts and agonistic promises, in our argument, can be seen in the light of Austin's theory of promises as performatives, because their utterance as speech acts (followed by written or electronic confirmation) is also the guarantee of their moral and legal capacity to bind the contracting actors together.

C. *Delayed promise.* A promise made by a company or a person who knows full well that they cannot meet the necessary conditions for its fulfillment, and therefore endlessly delays its lifespan. This can be seen as a sub-category of false promises. It is a model that fits well with the idea of the "unicorn": a startup that will generate profit in the ratio of millions in relation to the initial venture capital investment or purchase price. The investors who make these financial decisions, which are almost always in the tens of millions of dollars, belong to a new breed of wealthy speculative capitalists specializing in delayed promises. Another example of delayed promise is the ROI (return-on-investment) model, which describes a ratio between the net future profit and the current cost of investment of some resources.

That Silicon Valley has come to rely on delayed promises is made obvious by the fact that many of its most successful companies have failed to produce profits or have only became profitable after many years. Writing about Silicon Valley's "tolerance for failure," Adrian Daub reminds us that

> failing seems to carry opposite meanings depending on who does it. If a traditional brick-and-mortar business hemorrhages money as unregulated digital competition moves in, then that's just a sign that brick-and-mortar business deserves to die. By contrast, if a disruptive New Economy startup loses money by the billions, it's a sign of how revolutionary and bold they are. (2018, 23)

Within a discourse of "disruption" and "scalability," the promise for profit might be forever delayed.

It is important, however, to distinguish between bankers and venture capitalists (VCs): The first accrue debt, while the latter invest in equity of a startup and as such buy into the potential of its success. Unlike bankers, VCs are willing to fail and lose their investors' money. Success in this case means growing a company over a decade into a more highly valued one and then selling their equity share at a multiple of the initial investment. This is not necessarily a false promise, but rather a patient bet on a possible success. Losing money, in the case of VCs, is often seen as a temporary necessity that drives innovation. Still, this is an experiment whose results are delayed and uncertain. It also divides the economy into those who can afford to wait and those who cannot. VCs and investors know full well that they will have to wait years or even decades before they can enjoy the fruits of their success, while low- or middle-class citizens cannot afford to wait that long or risk losing their savings. We will return to this distinction between venture capital and banks in our discussion of the derivative form and the Great Recession in chapter 4.

At the same time, users who complain about slow products, limited battery life, or brittle hardware are answered with the promise that the problem will be fixed in the next model or "upgrade." Instead of being acknowledged as such, the failure is therefore co-opted into the business model of planned obsolescence and the inculcation of the constant need to upgrade their software and devices. Planned obsolescence and the delayed promise thus sustain and enable one another since the affective economy of planned obsolescence guarantees the endless temporal horizon of the delayed promise.

In chapters 3 and 4, we will further explore this set of promises by closely looking at buffering and derivatives. More specifically, we will unpack two failed promises: the promise of seamlessness and limitless access to information made by Silicon Valley, and the promise of prosperity made by Wall Street. In both cases, these failed promises set the ground for collective failure, as they push users into regimes of debt and anxiety propagated by an accumulation of unfulfilled promises.

The Promise of Convenience

For the 99 percent, seamless connectivity and monetary prosperity are yet to be materialized. Still, they function as dominant cultural fantasies, giving birth to the fetishization of "on-demand culture" or to the quasi-theological belief in the power of "the Market." The opaque systems of finance and tech both promise an enhanced convenience that, in turn, can improve our wellbeing and happiness. The underlying logic of this pursuit is that financial capital and technological breakthroughs can be used to surpass and extend bodily limitations. This (failed) promise, however, is nothing new. In *The Value of Convenience: A Genealogy of Technical Culture* (1993), Thomas Tierney demonstrates how the idea of "necessity" has been continually expanded throughout modernity. Due to growing dependency on technology, what once was a luxury has quickly regained the status of necessity – from automobiles to refrigerators and, recently, smartphones and constant WiFi connectivity. Tierney's work contributes to the centuries-long discussion of "biological needs" (food, clothing, shelter, and other factors needed for survival and reproduction) versus "social needs." As he proposes, "ancient necessity was primarily concerned with satisfying the *demands* of the body, while modern necessity is largely focused on overcoming *limits* which are imposed by the body" (1993, 30, original emphasis).

The ideology of instant gratification on which the digital economy is based creates new needs that, in turn, are recast as necessities. As Tierney's historical overview makes manifest, since the industrial revolution the value of convenience has become a dominant ideology. In the digital age, the assumption that life should be as convenient and pain-free as possible functions as a doxa. Uber, Seamless, and countless other mobile applications are first and foremost about convenience. In fact, the entire "gig economy" (studied in chapter 2) is based on the promise of convenience: you can sit and relax (or go to your day job) while an anonymous freelancer will take care of your house, pets, plants, or shopping. The proliferation of the gig economy exemplifies what Tierney describes as the main value of technology: mitigating the demands of the body, which are now seen as inconveniences. This leads to "a denial of the body and the temporal-spatial limits which are imposed by it" (1993, 191). This "ascetic tendency," to use Tierney's terminology, can now be seen in Netflix's revealing declaration that its only competitor is the user's need for sleep – and not other streaming services (Raphael 2017). This war on sleep cannot be detached from the urge to deny bodily limitations that even technology cannot (yet) mitigate. Our inability to binge-watch a series for 12 hours straight can be seen as a failure of our willpower or cognitive abilities. To avoid such judgment, we must train our eyes, brains, and muscular systems to consume information at an ever-growing pace.

But there is more at stake than the dangers of insufficient sleep or lack of exercise. Take, for example, Tierney's study of one of the most essential technologies of modernity: the automobile. With its promise of freedom and agency, the automobile paradoxically "binds people to the economic structure of modernity in a manner similar to that which bound the nineteenth-century homesteader" (1993, 110). For the vast majority of drivers, purchasing a car requires financial obligations that must be paid over time, such as loans, credit, and debt. While the promise of overcoming the speed limit of the human body is tempting, it has created an industry of debt, insurance, and risk – as well as devastating statistics of injuries and deaths. This is an early example of how technological innovations germinate financial infrastructures designed to increase inequality. More often than not, the promise of convenience, efficiency, and speed paradoxically produces painful regimes of failure.

As different as it is from the auto industry, digital technology can be seen as a direct continuation of the very same logic. It promises to eliminate distance by creating a "global village," while it effectively creates dependency on internet providers, cloud computing, server farms, content providers, and legislation. And while most users do not need to secure a loan in order to pay the monthly fees to internet providers, they have no control over the pacing of data transmission.

Even with the internet, the quest to eliminate biological needs is destined to fail. In fact, we are increasingly dependent on screens that require sedentary behaviors. The result, as described by Lauren Berlant, is sensory and cognitive exhaustion. Critiquing the so-called "obesity epidemic" in the United States, she writes that

> [t]he contemporary human is fatigued in the literal sense but also in a metaphorical one, as in what metal "feels" when it no longer can bear the stress placed on it. I will suggest that eating is like the "self-medicating" practices of drinking, sex, television, sports fandom, video games, and drugs, but not because they're addictive. (This varies, after all.) My claim is that these kinds of activities provide

opportunities to become absorbed in the present, opportunities that suffuse people with the pleasure of engaged appetites and enable people to feel more resilient in the everyday. This sense of resilience is different from actual resilience: bodies wear out from the pleasures that help them live on. But the growth of the appetite industries in a world where there is less time to enjoy them says something of the desperate need for relief provided by the pleasures that make it possible to get up tomorrow and do it all over again. (2010, 27)

By studying systemic failure in relation to exhaustion and sensory endurance, we hope to highlight the kind of negotiations necessary for survival in our entrepreneurial age. The next chapter will dive deeper into the pursuit of convenience by looking at mobile apps and studying the way they counterintuitively limit the conditions for creating and supporting social and communal bonds. Within the context of the ever-growing gig economy, they create a new tyranny in the link between appetites and applications.

Chapter 2

Creative Destruction and the New Socialities

Introduction

Building on our discussion of the promise of convenience, we argue in this chapter that new digital platforms and tools have sped up the experience of obsolescence and upgrading, and have thus created a new relationship between risk, innovation, failure, and futurity. Our further claim is that while this new relationship appears to expand possible social futures, the reality is that it threatens to shrink them. Our first step is to understand how failure has emerged as a slogan of entrepreneurial cultures in the digital era.

The paradox here is that while entrepreneurial disruptions in the digital era seem to profit from the virtues of new modes of sociality – and their apparent popularity and success – they actually rely on the failure or induced obsolescence of prior modes of sociality. Thus, the entrepreneurial multiplication of mobile apps and the "gig economy" they support enable the shrinkage of futures anchored in previous socialities. This is the dark side of the "creative destruction" that Schumpeter identified as the primary dynamic force of industrial capitalism. This process signals a new chapter in the commodification of sociality, whose earlier histories can be found in advertising and related modernist modes of mass consumption. Within this new economy of apps and digital platforms, failure plays a crucial role in isolating subjects from one another, creating feelings of self-blame and animosity. Paradoxically, these difficult notions make users ever more desperate to find and adopt services or apps promising to make their lives more convenient or to recreate a new sense of collective identity.

This chapter will therefore build on previous critiques of the "gig economy." Calling it "the future of American work," the American journalist Nathan Heller explains that

> The model goes by many names – the sharing economy; the gig economy; the on-demand, peer, or platform economy – but the companies share certain premises. They typically have ratings-based marketplaces and in-app payment systems. They give workers the chance to earn money on their own schedules, rather than through professional accession. And they find toeholds in sclerotic industries. (Heller 2017)

Bearing these characteristics in mind, we will offer a case study of Uber in order to unpack the ways in which this new economy reshapes social bonds.

This chapter, however, does not set out to form a hierocracy of social attachments, lamenting the days when one had to stop a taxi in the street instead of summoning an Uber with two clicks. This nostalgic longing too often idealizes a supposedly "pre-digital" world where strangers carpooled into the sunset or helped each other carry groceries from the local store. We propose to abandon the futile, and to a large extent inaccurate, comparison between "analog" and "digital" worlds and, instead, to study the ever-accelerating pace at which social bonds and collective networks are formed and quickly become obsolete. We do not reiterate clichéd notions of a communal paradise replaced by a profit-driven inferno. But by mapping the rapid, ongoing replacement of one such structure with another, we hope to move beyond existing critiques of the gig economy. Finally, we build on recent literature on the proliferation of the gig economy to further develop our understanding of failure. It is the failure to create stable, long-lasting social structures that we wish to link to the proliferation of mobile apps and their promise of convenience. What kinds of failures are perpetuated by the pursuit of convenience and immediacy? And what is the language used to dismiss them?

Innovation, Inc.

The virtues of failure (as we already suggested in our Introduction) are now fervently embraced by high-technology companies and business experts, especially in the United States. This fervor has its roots in the mid-twentieth-century discovery of innovation, risk, and even crisis. There is also a direct line from this embrace of innovation and volatility in capitalism to the peculiar centrality of potential failure in the recent design technologies of the post-industrial West. In the speculative world of Silicon Valley, as we will argue in this chapter, the Schumpeterian valorization of innovation combines with the contemporary designer's preoccupation with anticipating failure to produce such maxims as "fail early, fail often."

Failure is hence being transformed from a vice into a virtue by stressing its importance for innovation. A different approach could be found in the proclivity of large modern organizations to deny failure, to create a "closed loop" in which effects and causes are so tightly interwoven that when failure has to be confronted, it is handled as something external to the organization or its technology, and thus made easier to dismiss or ignore (Easterling 2016). This structural tendency toward the denial of failure can also be seen in the saturation of today's designed technologies by futurity and testing. Indeed, earlier interests in utility, convenience, and naturalness have given way to "a boundless receptivity to failure," thus rendering users into testers of a world of tools which exist only to fail and be modified, without cease (Tonkinwise 2016). Modern organizations thus have a bipolar relationship to failure, being obsessed with failure at the level of design but prone to denial and data-cleansing when it comes to the effects of the technologies they deploy in the world. This bipolarity has its roots in the important ideas of Schumpeter about technology and innovation.

Like Max Weber, Schumpeter believed that capitalism was as much a cultural form as it was an arrangement of technology and production. Like Marx, he argued that capitalism was powered by its own ceaseless compulsion to reinvent itself. He predicted that capitalism would collapse by the end of the twentieth century, a victim of the logic of creative destruction corrupted by corporate managerialism (Schumpeter 1942). In this prediction, as we now know, he was spectacularly wrong, but his insights into the logic of industrial capitalism are still highly relevant. The most important among these insights was his idea of "creative destruction," most fully developed in his classic study of *Capitalism, Socialism and Democracy* (1942). The essence of the idea of "creative destruction" was that capitalist firms compete with each other, and that in the race to make themselves more competitive than other firms, they seek new technologies, which typically come from entrepreneurs whose inventions are financed by canny investors. If these firms succeed in introducing these innovations into a profit-making strategy, they can achieve a temporary monopoly over the relevant market, thus forcing others to imitate or replicate their innovation. This process leads to a general abandonment of earlier methods of labor utilization, production, marketing, pricing, and distribution, which amounts to the "creative destruction" of the old technology by the new, and when the innovation is sufficiently radical, to a wholesale destruction of previous forms of work, society, and control. The creativity of capitalism is its ceaseless search for innovations (i.e., marketable inventions) that guarantees the destruction of prior modes of organizing economy and society. Hence, "creative destruction." Schumpeter could be seen as a technological determinist, but he saw entrepreneurial innovation as a multidimensional process, in which finance capital, inventors, and industrial capitalists came together in a contingent cultural process, which was not driven by technology alone.

Schumpeter believed that stasis (equilibrium) in the

market economy is a contradiction. Stasis or equilibrium would mean that the market economy had lost its intrinsic strength and dynamism, and instead reverted to a different type of economy, namely a socialist, centrally planned, and collective economy. The essence of the market economy is its constant endogenous renewal; in other words, innovation is intrinsic to the system and technical progress is endemic (Hoefle 2012).

Though, prima facie, Schumpeter appears to have been entirely mistaken about the self-destruction of capitalism, he may well have been right about the replacement of certain forms of sociality with others through innovation (usually in the form of new technologies or infrastructures). We can examine this reading of Schumpeter's pessimism by turning to Silicon Valley today, a milieu obsessively committed to innovation.

Schumpeter's Second Life in Silicon Valley

Silicon Valley is admired and envied throughout the world for the way in which it has captured and branded digital innovation. It stands as the counterpoint in American corporate culture to Wall Street, though Wall Street is heavily digitalized and Silicon Valley is always in need of finance capital. In American corporate culture, Silicon Valley has gained a justified reputation for monopolizing the best minds, technologies, and assets to push the envelope in regard to digital innovation. The giants of Silicon Valley are Google, Amazon, Apple, Facebook, and Microsoft, with a handful of other companies that are close to their astronomical scale of profits and cash balances. As demonstrated by Spencer E. Ante (2008), venture capitalism can be traced back to the 1950s, when Harvard Business School professor Georges Doriot established the first venture capital and private equity firm, American Research and Development Corporation (ARDC). The "Big Five," as Silicon Valley's giants are often called, now operate in a different economic landscape, where value-extraction is rewarded more highly than value-creation (Mazzucato 2016). When companies are driven to maximize shareholder value, the future is reimagined as a series of risks and opportunities (Beckert 2016).

Among the numerous innovations that have emerged from Silicon Valley in the last three decades, one of the most distinctive and wealth-producing has been in the domain of mobile apps, which allow end users to purchase a wide range of goods and services through their mobile phones with a high degree of speed, convenience, and reliability. The sector of the US economy that is now driven by apps can be measured by the combined valuation of more than 100 startups in this space, with revenues that are estimated to be worth more than $900 billion in 2018, according to one industry report estimating the combined value of consumer apps, enterprise apps, and app-driven Internet of Things (IoT) technologies (Stephens and Mahesh 2018). These impressive numbers are expected to grow, as over 28 billion devices have been added to the app-enabled IoT in 2018, supporting "smart-home" devices such as Google Assistant, thermostats, or vacuum cleaners like the Roomba (Stephens and Mahesh 2018).

While most digital services offer both an app and a website or digital platform, we wish to focus solely on mobile apps (rather than smart-home apps), as they offer a unique experience and ontology: they reside in mobile devices and are therefore personalized, password-protected, and easy to access. They follow users wherever they go, as long as they have access to a WiFi network. Furthermore, mobile access challenges earlier definitions of the digital divide. According to a 2017 Pew Research report,

> In 2016, one-fifth of adults living in households earning less than $30,000 a year were 'smartphone-only' internet users – meaning they owned a smartphone but did not have broadband internet at home ... In contrast, only 4% of those living in households earning $100,000 or more fell into this category in either year. (Anderson 2017)

In short, due to fewer options for online access at their disposal, many lower-income Americans are relying more on smartphones. However, while hundreds of new apps are introduced to the market and made available on a daily basis, not everyone can download and use them. In 2018, over 30 million Americans were excluded from the app economy because they were unable to pay for data (Stephens and Mahesh 2018).

While messaging and social media apps such as Facebook, WhatsApp, and Instagram boast billions of monthly active users, the number of mobile apps is rising exponentially. Within this new economy, ride-sharing, food delivery, or other task-oriented apps are often hailed as empowering, efficient, and user-friendly. Renowned publications such as *Forbes* and *The New York Times*, for example, touted gig economy apps such as Uber, Airbnb, and TaskRabbit as paving the way for a possible solution to unemployment (Kessler 2018). A 2013 *Forbes* cover story described the gig economy as "an economic revolution that is quietly turning millions into part-time entrepreneurs" (Kessler 2018, 61). As Sarah Kessler (2018), Greg Goldberg (2018), Alex Rosenblat (2018a), and many others have recently demonstrated, this description could not have been further from the truth.

Since 2013, when class-action lawsuits against Uber and Lyft were extensively covered in the press, there has been a backlash against the so-called "gig economy" (Goldberg 2018). Instead of a potential means for the empowerment of both workers and users, it has been described as "the deployment of technology to intensify inequality, in this case by creating monopolies that aggregate and co-opt the effort and resources of many users, who are pitted against one another within the platforms" (Horning 2014). While we find these strong criticisms highly credible, we would like to offer a different entryway into to the study of the app economy.

The crucial feature of this new economic space, we argue, is that it is focused on the end customer in two distinct ways. The first is the harnessing of mobile connectivity to allow users to purchase a remarkably wide range of services (ranging from limousines and taxis, to therapeutic services, food deliveries, movie tickets, dog-walking, house-cleaning, air tickets, entertainment discounts, and more) by acquiring an app on their handheld devices that is usually free. The truly radical aspect of this economy is the role it assigns to the consumer in the constant refinement, improvement, friendliness, and cost of the services on offer, all based in a design innovation which goes by the rubric "UX" or "user experience," in which constant feedback from users is drawn upon to refine the app on an almost continuous basis. This is very different from market research based on focus groups, traditional demographic analysis, or even the study of patterns in "big data" about consumption. UX makes customers themselves a part of the design process and turns user experience into the primary site of design interest for the service provider. We are no longer just "users": we have become testers, analysts, and feedback providers at the very heart of real-time design improvement. Thus, despite the fact that endless apps will quickly become obsolete, there is no such thing as an absolute "failure" in the world of mobile apps. Instead, the app economy relies on an endless communication loop between end user and product designer, so that each failure is simply the driver of the next improvement. The result is a rapid need for "upgrades" that requires the user to learn something new, so that he or she can be an even better source of "experience" to help drive the next iteration of the mobile app (Tonkinwise 2016). As we argued in chapter 1, this is a "delayed promise" in the purest sense.

Second, within the new gig economy the consumer pays for a service rather than for any particular employee, producing a growing sense of depersonalization and randomness. Instead of enabling millions to become "part-time entrepreneurs" overnight, mobile apps offer transitory, impersonal encounters that are almost immediately quantified by the consumer ("Thanks for using Uber! How many stars will you give Lorena?"). This endless quantification is what sets the gig economy apart from earlier service work such as waitressing, delivery, or taxi driving.

With its dependence on surveillance and the exploitation of temporary workers (often referred to as "suppliers" or "partners" by the companies employing them in order to avoid providing them social benefits, health insurance, or job security), the gig economy has been the focus of many alarmist studies (Goldberg 2018; Rosenbalt 2018a). Bearing these concerns in mind, we would like to connect its growing popularity to a new development in economics called "evolutionary economics." This term, first used by Thorstein Veblen (1898), describes technological innovation as the key driver of profit and wealth, and places such innovation in a long view of human evolution. This approach is not yet a part of mainstream economics, though it has been gaining legitimacy in recent years. In this approach, equilibrium is not seen as either the ideal aim or the driving principle of human economies. In their place, change, incessant disturbance, and evolution are seen as the key drivers of the economy. The ideas of Charles Darwin, including those of adaptation, selection, and survival, play important roles in evolutionary economics, and Schumpeter is seen as one of the giants of this approach to economic organizations and economic change. Innovation in the process of competition among firms in industrial capitalism is a key element of the struggle to survive, and losers (as well as losing arrangements of technology, work, and social life) are doomed to disappear while more "adaptive" survivors are promised to dominate, until they too become dysfunctional in terms of the environment. In this view, adaptation means innovation and survival means market domination (at least for some time). As disturbance and disruption are at the heart of evolutionary economics, it is no surprise that, in the last few decades, the biggest application of Schumpeterian ideas to the present corporate environment has come from the idea of "disruption," first coined by Bower and

Christensen (1995), as the cardinal virtue of successful corporations, entrepreneurs, and CEOs.

Within this celebratory discourse of disruption, failure functions as a new kind of commodity. It is being monetized by Silicon Valley in three distinct ways: First, by a system of A/B testing in which every consumer choice is monitored and used to sort users into "taste clusters" that, in turn, enable algorithmic recommender systems to try and predict what users might like in the future (Alexander 2016). To that extent, even a "no choice" such as leaving the app or turning off the device holds value, as it implies that the user was disappointed by the choices presented to her, and will thus require a round of improvements and further A/B testing. Second, most mobile apps can be downloaded free of charge, as their business model is based on charging commissions, "premium fees," or both, from users. What users therefore receive is often a partial, limited, and strategically "failed" version of the service whose sole purpose is to convince them to sign up for a monthly subscription. This model could be found in mobile apps as different as Spotify (for music), Headspace (for mindfulness), and Tinder (for dating). Third, apps are strategically designed to be as addictive as possible, maximizing "time-on-device" (TOD), a term originally used to describe slot machines in casinos (Schüll 2014). Natasha Dow Schüll's exploration of "the machine's zone" – an endlessly repetitive sphere in which "time, space, and social identity are suspended" (2014, 13) – enables us to unpack the fantasy of empowerment and convenience sustained by mobile apps. While these systems produce a sense of limitless, seamless, and personalized choice, they paradoxically "function to narrow choices, disconnect, and gain exit from the self" (Schüll 2014). In short, these apps are most successful when users fail to control themselves, spending money they don't have or texting 40 different Tinder profiles in one night.

One of the most distinctive features of the mobile-app economy, and the one which major investors seek to identify early, is the app's potential for large "network effects" (Jervis forthcoming). Network effects refer to the increase in the value of the tool to any user because of increased usage (by the addition of other users). It is important to note that network effects are different from virality, as virality simply refers to the speed and scale of a tool (not to the value increase to any and all users from additional users). Nor is the network effect another term for better connectivity among users or for economies of scale, as the latter refers to cost reduction by increases in production. Rather, these effects index the positive effect of the increase of users (say of Uber, or Instagram, or Reddit, or TaskRabbit) on the experience of each user of the tool. Network effects are usually crucial to "sharing economies." The most profitable innovations in the world of mobile apps thus rely on some sort of social insight (and not solely or necessarily on a technological breakthrough) that permits the innovator to create or expand network effects. As we will argue in the following section, this ideology, which places the highest value on identifying and investing in "network effects," has profound implications for human sociality. As we will demonstrate in our analysis of Uber, the obsession with maximizing the network effect produces several kinds of failure. To preserve and increase the rate of growth, moments of failure (such as lack of a support system for Uber drivers, or their need to deal with intoxicated or violent passengers) are at times cut out of the system by algorithms or bots. This is done unequally and opaquely, in ways that erode social bonds between customers and service providers, as well as between customers and other customers.

Rethinking the Social: Convenience, Connectivity, Identity

We can see the Schumpeterian creative destruction of prior forms of sociality in the ways in which our digital devices, applications, and services have an interconnected impact on convenience, connectivity, and identity. Connectivity is, of course, the technological *sine qua non* of all the new user-based, mobility-oriented applications that define consumer life in the West and in many other societies, to varying degrees. Connectivity is the new ideology of sociality as a whole. The ubiquity of words such as "network," "friend," "viral," "influencer," "crowd-sourcing," and many more, indicates the extent to which the new app economy has begun to erode earlier frameworks of connectivity, which were more closely tied to geography, social location, intimacy, memory, biography, and personal idiosyncrasy.

The term "connectivity" holds at least two meanings: 1. "Connectivity" to the internet and to digital infrastructures; 2. "Connectivity" between humans and machines, humans and other humans, or machines and other machines. When referring to the first category, it is crucial to distinguish "connectivity" from "accessibility":

Even for those who may have nominal access to information, there are barriers to full engagement in the information society. These barriers exist not only in terms of connection but also in terms of awareness needed to be able to engage in symbolic manipulation of information and the purposive nature of that information for social cohesion (personal and public). In fact, it can be argued that a superficial connectivity perversely accentuates the condition of the unconnected. (Baker et al. 2013, 4)

Ownership of a WiFi-connected mobile device, therefore, should not be equated with user empowerment, control, or knowledge. At the same time, taglines such as "connecting people" are frequently used by social media companies like Facebook to mask their contribution to genocide, mass violence, and the increased risk of depression among its users (Lin et al. 2016; Mozur 2018).

Of course, this new mode of creative destruction also has technology at its core and has vast economic effects. But its massive value creation, surplus extraction, and exploitation is based on sociality itself as its primary and exploitable raw material. These momentous shifts in connectivity are also intensified by changes in personhood and in the ideology of convenience. In chapter 1, we already remarked on the deep links between modern consumerist ideology and the hegemony of the idea of convenience. In the digital era, this long-standing disposition is deepened by new modes of connectivity and of what we used to call identity. Connectivity and convenience develop a new affinity that is based on the idea that the valuable conveniences are those that depend on both social and WiFi connectivity and that the connectivity that is most valued is the one that promotes convenience (the most powerful example being the status of Amazon as a planetary corporate giant). Moreover, connectivity today encompasses not only anthropomorphic behaviors but also a growing dependence on bots, algorithms, and nonhuman agents. Instead of "connecting people," it might be more accurate to describe the app economy as "connecting people to other people and/or machines without always being able to tell them apart." This "politics of the proxy," to use Hito Steyerl's important term (2014), creates a digital world in which it is gradually impossible to distinguish humans from automated bots.

This important development can explain why neither connectivity nor convenience would be linked as powerfully in our digital times if it were not for a tectonic shift in the classical idea of identity, which allows for the massification of what we call (following Deleuze) "dividuals." In an earlier work by Appadurai (2015), he identified what he called "predatory dividuation," that is the breakdown of individuals into a series of scores, ranks, features, attributes, and dimensions, which were relevant and useful for the production of immense profits by the financial industries. This decomposition of the individual is crucial for risk ratings, credit scores, consumer profiling, and other operations on which contemporary finance depends. This process has been remarked in different ways by various critical theorists, some of whom recognize the prescience of Gilles Deleuze in identifying the emergence of the "dividual" as a new sort of capitalist subject (Pasquale 2016; Cheney-Lippold 2017). There is a growing recognition that the reduction of the "individual" to the "dividual" is a momentous development, which signals the end of a central idea of Western modernity in which personality, agency, motivation, interest, and the body were encased in a single envelope, for which we are habituated to using the term "individual." This individual was earlier regarded as both the central agent of property regimes (through possessive individualism), the key bearer of rights in liberal democratic discourse, and the irreducible ground of ethical action and responsibility. Without this idea of the individual, Western modernity loses its most critical presumption.

By "dividualizing" human beings, by making certain (often numerical) dimensions of the individual more important than the total assemblage that used to be the individual, contemporary finance (as we shall show in our analysis of the corrosive workings of the derivative markets in chapter 4) changes the nature of human subjectivity to make it easier to aggregate, recombine, monitor, predict, and exploit subjects for the purposes of financial markets, primarily by making scorable and rankable "dividuals" the sources of debt. To incur debt, you need no special ethical, biological, or racial capacities. You need to be a debt-worthy dividual.

For John Cheney-Lippold, this is part of a shift into a world of "algorithmic identities":

In a period of time only slightly longer than the average television commercial break, you will have generated, through your web activity, an identity that is likely separate from the person who you thought you were. In a database far, far away, you have been assigned a gender, ethnicity, class, age, education level, and potentially the status of parent with x number of children ... Who we are in this world is much more than a straightforward declaration of self-identification or intended performance. Who we are, following internet researcher Greg Elmer's work on "profiling machines," is also a declaration by our data as interpreted by algorithms. We are ourselves, plus layers upon additional layers of what I have previously referred to as algorithmic identities. (2017, 3–5)

These new algorithmic identities reshape our understanding of social structures as they effectively blur the lines between humans and bots. One result of this complex shift is a growing dehumanization of service providers such as drivers, cleaners, or delivery workers, as users grow more accustomed to communicating with bots and algorithmic systems. Moreover, the gig economy also sustains a system of exploitation and information asymmetry, as a brief analysis of Uber will demonstrate.

"Partners" – Not "Employees"

Launched in 2010, Uber's promise to "Earn Money by Driving or Get a Ride Now" has radically changed the urban landscape in major cities around the world. As journalist Nikil Saval (2019) lamented,

Uber has devastated traditional taxi services, chiefly by operating outside the bounds that regulate those services, such as licensing requirements that cap the number of cars a company can own. Because it enjoys the subsidy of venture capital, Uber does not need to make a profit; in fact, it loses billions every year.

While the company offers a fantasy of convenience, it is responsible for a significant increase in traffic delays in over 22 cities in the United States (Saval 2019). Worse still, it has been producing what Saval describes as an eradication of social and communal responsibilities. Once ordering a ride, the passenger transforms the urban space into a sterile environment not unlike a video game. In Saval's words,

> Everything is evacuated from the picture except for streets: there is nothing standing between you and the vehicle but time and empty space. For a consumer, the image is ethereal. But the streets are actually full of buildings, people, and other cars. Getting around in a city requires taking up space, which by nature is subject to scarcity. *Every new passenger diminishes the experience for the existing pool of customers.* (2019, emphasis added)

Saval and others have warned that the rising popularity of Uber reduces bus and rail ridership, increases gas emissions, and changes the public sphere. While these concerns focus on commuters, other recent studies provided an alarmist account of Uber's impact on its drivers. Studying Uber's algorithmic management, Luke Stark and Alex Rosenblat mapped the company's remote management console and the ways in which it helps to make more efficient use of driver time in this digital "matching market" (Stark and Rosenblat 2016). The result, they argue, is fundamental informational asymmetries between the worker and the platform owner:

> For example, drivers have about 15 seconds to accept ride requests via the platform, and are not shown the rider's destination. With drivers in the dark, they don't know when they will accept short, unprofitable fares. Meanwhile, Uber furthers its own goal of providing near-instantaneous service to all prospective riders. Because Uber designs the

platform and can change it at will, conflicts of interest between worker and platform owner are systematically settled in favor of Uber via the platform itself, not collective bargaining or other processes that allow for worker participation. (Stark and Rosenblat 2016, 3762)

To push this argument further, we should remember that there are other conflicts of interest at play: not only between Uber and its drivers (which the company refuses to define as "employees" and, instead, refers to as "partners" or "suppliers") – but also between passengers and drivers, as well as between passengers and other passengers. When using a popular feature such as "Uber Pool," which matches riders with other riders heading in the same direction for a cheaper fare, any additional rider will result in a delay. With their surveillance and opaque penalty system, as well as their recasting of additional riders as a direct threat to one's efficiency and time management, they transform the daily commute into a highly individualized, quantifiable, and game-like experience.

This can explain why ride-share apps like Uber or Lyft are substantially different from earlier forms of capitalist exploitation. Building on Stark and Rosenblat's research, the 2017 AI Now Report proposes that

The task for researchers is to determine specifically what makes AI-powered asymmetries different from other forms of monitoring, such as Taylorist scientific management and the audit culture of total quality control. One clear difference is AI's reliance on workplace surveillance and the data it produces, and thus the normalization of workplace surveillance. (Campolo et al. 2017, 10)

Returning to the discussion of convenience in chapter 1 as that which can be used to surpass and extend bodily limitations (Tierney 1993), the case of Uber demonstrates how this pursuit of instant gratification has germinated new forms of exhaustion and sensory endurance. Drivers are dangerously lured to stay on the road for hours by using algorithmic systems such as "surge pricing" or tools like notifications and rewards. Not only is their ability to unionize, rest, or form solidarity with other drivers compromised due to their dependence on algorithmic "bosses," but any failure to obey these new tyrants will result in "deactivation" and exclusion from the platform.

When something goes wrong, drivers are left to fend for themselves by calling or writing "community support," a misleading euphemism for Uber's automated service center. As Rosenblat describes, this often worsens tensions between the drivers and the platform:

> Cecily McCall, an African-American driver from Pompano Beach, Fla., told me that a passenger once called her "dumb" and "stupid," using a racial epithet, so she ended the trip early. She wrote to a support rep to explain why and got what seemed like a robotic response: "We're sorry to hear about this. We appreciate you taking the time to contact us and share details." (2018b)

An attempt to report a failure can therefore quickly backfire, as social or communal systems of accountability are replaced by black-box algorithms. Once again, the denial of failure is achieved by changing the terms by which it is described:

> While critics use the language of the workplace to describe the treatment of drivers, the language of technology can

deflect such concerns. When payments for trips are missing, labor advocates might call it wage theft, but Uber says it's a glitch. When Uber charges passengers what it predicts they are willing to pay based on their route rather than standard rates, economists may call it price discrimination, but Uber explains it as an innovation in artificial intelligence. (Rosenblat 2018b)

The failure we are most interested in is therefore not the precariousness of working for an algorithmic "boss"; it is, rather, the language used to market this transition to both drivers and riders as a cutting-edge "innovation in artificial intelligence." The promise for enhanced productivity, freedom, and control over one's time is once again delayed. Yet this delay is denied and masked as a "disruption," reviving Schumpeter's creative destruction without acknowledging its ever-increasing price.

At the same time, the anxiety being perpetuated by the app economy does not result solely from fears of job loss or from job precariousness due to increased automation or the "Uberfication" of the job market. Instead, it reflects much deeper, and often denied, concerns about "the dissolution of social bonds" (Goldberg 2018, 13). When comparing carpooling to Uber, for example, it is easy to attend to the idea that the former is in some ways better than the latter. Summarizing the criticisms of the "sharing economy," Goldberg provides us with an example of their binary and somewhat superficial approach to these complex processes: For these critics, "carpoolers come to form a miniature, self-governing community, ethical and altruistic where Uber is exploitative, self-serving, antisocial" (2018,

151). Resisting such binary divisions between altruistic and agonistic, good and bad, we wish to end this chapter with a reminder that previous employment models, especially in industries such as taxis or hotels, were no less precarious and exploitative.

Furthermore, it will be a mistake to theorize Uber drivers as an ignorant or helpless mass prone to exploitation. In practice, researchers studying online forums operated by drivers have revealed the extent to which they are able to resist and manipulate some aspects of the app's algorithmic management. This can be achieved, for example, by blocking the system (e.g. rejecting platform instructions and refusing to carry out requested jobs), or by switching between alternative ride-hailing platforms and apps such as Uber, Lyft, Juno, or Via in order to maximize profits and compare the attractiveness of rides (Möhlmann and Zalmanson 2017). Another method of resistance is "gaming the system" – searching for loopholes that drivers could exploit to their own advantage such as canceling rides to avoid negative ratings by angry customers (Möhlmann and Zalmanson 2017). In short, the relationship between drivers and the platform is more complex and dynamic than it seems.

Conclusion: The Fantasy of "Opting Out"

We have argued that the world of digital innovation has made a large contribution to the destruction of older socialities, by radically changing and reassembling the meanings of convenience, identity, and connectivity. We can see now that this massive transformation in the nature of sociality also converges with the predatory "dividualization" that is central to the operations of contemporary financialized capitalism. Such dividuation is also evident in other spaces of the digital world, such as streaming, profiling, targeted advertising, and surveillance. In theory, the new regimes of the social can also legitimately be resisted by those who maintain a deliberately "antisocial" posture, which resists the new digital regimes of surveillance, connectivity, and e-bonding. However, as we will argue in our Conclusion, opting out of the digital ecosystem is more a fantasy than a reality, and a surveillance-free life is impossible to obtain (Brunton and Nissenbaum 2015). This generalized suspicion about sociality is intensified in an age in which surveillance, marketing, and profiling have gone quite far in eroding any form of collective resistance.

Pushing against any notion of technological determinism, we must stress that it is not the app or the mobile technology that is to be blamed for the obsolescence of socialities; it is the "creative destruction" that has monstrously morphed into an industry poised to monetize the margins of its already existing business models by turning every failure into a commodity.

Both in the realm of digital connectivity and in the domain of debt-driven financial markets, failure plays a key reproductive role, for it is presented as a normal part of life in the world of apps and debt. In the Conclusion to this book, we will return to the question of what sort of progressive politics might still be possible in the age of the digitized dividual. In the next chapter, we return to our definition of "habitual failure" in order to develop a detailed argument about the monetization of waiting and the workings of ignorance about the black boxes that shape everyday life. The key example for these links is buffering, a moment of lag often ignored or forgotten.

Chapter 3
Failure, Forgotten: On Buffering, Latency, and the Monetization of Waiting

Introduction

Following our analysis of mobile apps and the rapid obsolescence of social structures, this chapter will demonstrate how technological failure is being monetized. We will look at buffering and other moments of latency and digital lag not as technical problems awaiting a solution but, rather, as strategic tools in creating dependence on internet service providers (ISPs) and digital infrastructures. That buffering is rarely discussed outside the framework of net-neutrality debates or infrastructural decisions is an indication of the role that memory plays in our judgment of failure. Our main question therefore is not how and when will buffering be eliminated, but why is buffering being forgotten? The answer draws on an analysis of habit and memory, unpacking why users are quick to dismiss and ignore the many mischiefs and digital stammer of their beloved gadgets. It also recasts buffering and lag as a delayed promise of seamlessness. Within an economic and cultural discourse hailing infinite connectivity, buffering can potentially remind users that new media are precarious and unreliable. Its systemic denial is therefore crucial for sustaining the logic and business model of Silicon Valley.

To do so, this chapter connects the following discussion of buffering, disconnection, and latency to longer traditions of information theory and cybernetics. Information theorists such as Norbert Wiener and Claude Shannon failed to agree on a definition of noise: the former considered noise to be the opposite of signal, whereas the latter considered noise as integral to the process of "selecting" a message (Wiener 1965; Shannon and Weaver 1975). Shannon and Weaver's famous diagram (originally titled "A Mathematical Theory of Communication") foregrounds the importance of noise to communication systems (Shannon and Weaver 1975). Arguably, noise is a failure in perception, yet also the opposite is true: signal is a perceived successful structuring or ordering of noise. In this model, noise always exists and is sometimes filtered away as such. But what happens when we grow accustomed to (unfiltered) noise? How can we theorize visual noise that – despite its ubiquity – is seldom discussed or studied by media scholars?

Drawing on our discussion of "techno-failure" in chapter 1, we would like to use buffering as a case study for the aesthetics and logics of failure. But first, a definition is in order. The notorious "loading" GIF (which is often referred to as "the spinning wheel of death") appears on screen every time an internet server preloads data onto a reserved area of memory known as "the buffer." As defined by the *Oxford English Dictionary* (OED), a "buffer" can be "a person or thing that prevents incompatible or antagonistic people or things from harming each other." The word "buffer" therefore invokes a tension between contingency and control. In digital networks, the buffer is the part that delays transmission so that there is enough data for the streaming to occur without interruption. Ironically, the same mechanism meant to prevent disruptions and protect us from harmful contact has come to function as a constant source of anxiety and frustration. The result is a ubiquitous image: a never-ending, loopic, perpetual circle that occasionally bears the word "loading" beneath it. This GIF informs us that the streamed world in which we were immersed only seconds ago has now been put on hold, while the data is sent from one server to the next. This "aesthetics of lag," to use Nicole Starosielski's description of the endless instances in which web-based content is not efficiently transmitted, complicates our understanding of immediacy, agency, and control in the age of connected viewing (Starosielski 2015).

Building on our discussion of techno-failure and on the previous work of one of us (Alexander 2017), we propose that streaming services and compression technologies are inherently imbued with "digital dams": various disruptions and noises resulting from technological, legal, industrial, economic, or political structures and limitations. These moments are fundamentally different from earlier forms of spectatorial "noise" such as the distortion and degeneration of the VHS tape (Hilderbrand 2009), the "clunky" experience of the DVD (Smith 2008), or the commercial break on television and its "aesthetics of disruption and pollution"

(Jacobs 2011, 255). While the latter phenomena have been richly studied and theorized, buffering, bandwidth, limited battery life, and other "digital dams" have yet to receive the scholarly attention they deserve. As we shall see, they challenge the distinction between failure and breakdown discussed in previous chapters.

This scholarly lacuna is especially surprising considering the ubiquity of noise and disruption in digital systems. In fact, "streaming" as a concept has often been associated with efficiency, immediacy, and flow, and celebrated as a new means to shift control from content-makers and providers to viewers (Jenkins 2006). If we were to believe Netflix's CEO Reed Hastings, "waiting is dead" (quoted in Hass 2013).

In practice, however, the average growth in bandwidth (sometimes referred to as "Nielsen's Law of Internet Bandwidth") is slower than the growth in computational power (Moore's law), a fact that might increase users' encounter with "digital dams" in the future. Based on over 20 years of monitoring bandwidth, Danish engineer and inventor Jakob Nielsen warns that "bandwidth will remain the gating factor in the experienced quality of using the internet medium" (2018). Average bandwidth increases relatively slowly as telecoms companies try to avoid spending billions of dollars on infrastructure and equipment, and even once they do, it takes time to update their highly complex physical networks. More importantly,

> users are reluctant to spend much money on bandwidth ... If you buy twice as fast a modem, then you don't download web pages twice as fast: the speed of the internet is a function of both the individual user's connectivity and of the

infrastructure. You don't get the full benefits of your own bandwidth upgrades immediately – only gradually as the internet and the host servers improve. (Nielsen 2018)

Considering the fact that its global user base is growing exponentially, the image of the internet as a seamlessly accessible infrastructure is therefore far from the truth. This is further complicated by the existence of various digital divides. As Faye Ginsburg (2008), Helga Tawil-Souri (2017), Shannon Mattern (2019), and others have demonstrated, digital infrastructures are shaped by fiscal, political, and territorial interests that leave millions around the world with either limited or no access to the internet. Furthermore, ownership of a mobile phone does not guarantee access to information. As of 2018, 34 million Americans were unable to use the internet because they lack access to broadband or are unable to pay for data (Stephens and Mahesh 2018). This new class divide, however, is rarely mentioned in the debates on technological progress and the promise to build faster infrastructures.

In order to move away from utopian notions of connectivity, it is essential to stress that waiting is a relative term; it can mean something different based on different expectations and circumstances (Tawil-Souri 2017). In parts of the world where grids fail regularly, users "wait" for media quite differently, or they use different media (like cassettes, which still require rewinding). As explained in chapter 2, it is crucial to distinguish "connectivity" from "accessibility" (Baker et al. 2013, 4). Thinking about the often unacknowledged correlations between connectivity and class, race, disability, nationality, or age can help us explore "digital dams" behind the confines of Infrastructure Studies by studying political censorship, interface design, or biased algorithmic systems (like Google's AutoComplete, advertisements, or search results). And while buffering is a routine and much-expected phenomenon in countries or places without high-speed internet, it demands a different reading and theorization when encountered within the broader discourse of civic involvement and users' agency in highly connected Western countries.

Ignoring these digital divides, the dominant discourse surrounding bandwidth and connectivity is still mostly celebratory – focusing on ever-faster infrastructures such as 5G networks (which will be discussed below) or hailing compression technologies. As a result, buffering has either been ignored or described in terms of a transitory nuisance – a problem awaiting a solution. Its study has been mostly limited to IT journals or to the industry trade press, ignoring the phenomenology and affective economy created by digital noise and the liminality of waiting. In recent years, these technical and empirical analyses inspired either data-driven examination of bandwidth, latency, and internet protocols, or myriad essays on net neutrality and legislation (especially following the Netflix–Comcast deal signed in February 2015). Building on these investigations, we will extend our analysis of the promise machine to foreground the inherent failures and limitations of digital technologies. This will serve to problematize the commercial and institutional logic that hails the internet as the last stage of the information age – a utopian network offering immediacy, personalization, and choice.

The Myth of Immateriality

Similar to the opaque and highly specialized discourse of financial markets and economic infrastructures (which we will study in chapter 4), the discourse surrounding digital culture is based on abstraction and dematerialization. Building on Marx's diagnosis of capital as fetish, Wendy Hui Kyong Chun writes that "we 'primitive folk' worship source code as a magical entity – as a source of causality – when in truth the power lies elsewhere, most importantly in social and machinic relations" (2008, 301). In his 2011 essay "Current screens," Sean Cubitt offers his own comparison of the capital and digital architecture:

> As is typical of information capitalism, key brands like Apple, Matsushita, and Sony do not manufacture components themselves, and frequently do not even own the assembly plants where the final products come together. Instead they concentrate on the core business of intellectual property: trademarking the brand, patenting hardware, and copyrighting interlinked software and content. (2011, 25)

Immateriality is thus the prominent business model on which the digital industry is based, while the hazardous material conditions under which mobile devices and electronic consumer products are being produced are mostly outsourced to the Global South and remain hidden from the user (Mantz 2008).

This abstraction is communicated by using myriad metaphors that draw on the so-called pre-digital world. While "streams" and "clouds" refer to the natural world, devices and objects such as routers or servers are often anthropomorphized to a surprising degree. Netflix's official technology blog, for example, describes the company's inoperative servers as "unhealthy" rather than "dysfunctional" or "broken." Most posts published on the Netflix blog are anonymously written in the form of a "problem story": at first, a technical problem like buffering, latency, or "deviant servers" is introduced; then, the writer presents the company's most recent solution; finally, the tech-savvy readers are reminded that Netflix is always on the lookout for new employees ("If you would like to join us in tackling these kinds of challenges, we are hiring!"). Paradoxically, while these posts reveal the extent to which computer engineers and web-masters tend to anthropomorphize the digital infrastructure and describe it in terms of a biological body, their proposed solution is always based on the magic words "machine learning" and "automation."

These posts are far from anecdotes. In fact, they reveal the connection between digital noise (caused by "unhealthy servers") and the obsession with automation and efficiency, which is crucial to the denial of techno-failure. Whereas machines are occupying the place of engineers and developers, users are left with a discourse of constant progress that recognizes the existence of failure only within a broader narrative of problem-solving, automation, and artificial intelligence. This tendency to recast failure as a stepping stone on the way to success could also be found in another understudied literary genre: the annual investor letters, which convey perhaps even more authentically the real "thinking" and "authentic language" of Silicon Valley's corporate leadership. In the case of Amazon, for example, the annual shareholder letter written by Jeff Bezos since his company's IPO in 1997 has been providing a glimpse into the corporate embrace of failure by a company that didn't turn a consistent and substantial profit for most of its existence. In his 2010 letter, when the company was still losing money, Bezos portrayed a model based on innovation and experimentation:

All the effort we put into technology might not matter that much if we kept technology off to the side in some sort of R&D department, but we don't take that approach. Technology infuses all of our teams, all of our processes, our decision-making, and our approach to innovation in each of our businesses. It is deeply integrated into everything we do. (Quoted in Hooda 2017)

Putting his trust in technological progress, Bezos's annual letters promote the logic of "solutionism" (Morozov 2013) – the idea that given the right code, algorithms, or robots, technology can solve every problem, effectively making life "frictionless" and fulfilling its promise of convenience.

In practice, the discourse of "solutionism" and digital immateriality serves to deny the ubiquity of digital dams while maintaining the illusion that buffering is the exception rather than the rule. The problem of buffering can supposedly be solved by "upgrading" our devices, subscriptions, or data packages. Ignoring the various digital divides discussed in the Introduction, industry leaders such as Netflix's Hastings contest that buffering is destined to disappear entirely in the near future thanks to improved infrastructure and the advent of more efficient compression algorithms. This almost-religious belief in the myth of endless technological progress (as encompassed, among many other ways, in Moore's Law) is problematic in three ways: First, it misidentifies delay as a strictly technical issue while denying the extent to which infrastructure and web access are controlled by a multilayered network of private and governmental agencies; second, it fails to consider how waiting can be monetized and how deliberately slowing down access to the web can force consumers to opt for "premium services"; and third, it fetishizes compression as an ideal, problem-free solution to the ever-growing need for storage and transmission solutions.

The third aspect is particularly disturbing, as video compression is based by definition on several forms of erasure and selection. As defined by Lev Manovich, compression is "the technique of making image files smaller by deleting some information" (2002, 54). Furthermore, the transmission of digital data is based on "lossy compression": "[W]hile in theory computer technology entails the flawless replication of data, its actual use in contemporary society is characterized by loss of data, degradation, and noise" (2002, 55).

This process requires the elimination of supposedly "redundant" data while envisioning an imagined, "distracted listener" or viewer consuming content in "less-than-ideal conditions" (Sterne 2012, 2). Jonathan Sterne reminds us that while techno-utopias and the myth of progress go hand in hand with the promise of greater verisimilitude, the result is often a considerable loss of original data. The presence of noise is therefore *essential rather than accidental*, both in terms of compression techniques and standardized formats, and in the actual transmission protocols and packet switching. Paradoxically, the obsession with higher resolution and increasing bandwidth has led to an economy of "poor images" – the misspelled or anonymous viral JPEG, video file, or GIF that "has been expelled from the sheltered paradise that cinema seems to have once been" (Steyerl 2009).

In other words, there is a widening gap between the myths and metaphors surrounding and sustaining "on-demand culture" and "connected viewing" (Holt and Sanson 2013) and the users' daily experiences. We are led to believe that digital data is simultaneously "everywhere" and "nowhere," while the sad truth is that we can seamlessly consume audiovisual content only if we happen to live in a developed nation, pay premium fees for high-speed internet connectivity, and make sure we are surfing the web within a specified and limited distance of our increasingly fetishized routers and WiFi hotspots. And even when we are lucky enough to enjoy the impressive content libraries of streaming services like Netflix or Hulu, we often pay a price in the form of ambiguous privacy settings. While this chapter cannot examine the ongoing debate on privacy and surveillance in the digital age, we should bear in mind that streaming technology is partially based on "data-mining" methods that force us into a Faustian contract: "you're getting a free service, and the cost is information about you" (Pariser 2012, 6). At the same time, it would be a mistake to assume that seamless transmission is the only, or ultimate, goal of media conglomerates. In fact, slowing, limiting, or eliminating access to data might prove a much more effective way to monetize digital services.

False Latency and the Monetization of Waiting

Buffering introduces both slowness and hesitation to digital spectatorship – two factors that can be translated into various forms of capital. An analysis of buffering can therefore reveal how failure is being monetized by the tech industry. As market leaders such as Amazon and Google learned the hard way, faster data transmission rates produce lower tolerance of latency and delay. This is a result of users' growing dependency on WiFi: During the 1990s the internet was mostly used for static web browsing or email, activities that can tolerate delays. Today, however, video streaming and multi-player gaming – which require high bandwidth – are the most prevalent activities online. In the digital marketplace, even imperceptible delays can result in a loss of revenue: Amazon, for example, found that for every 100 milliseconds of delay on their site, they lose one percent of revenue. In fact, these sorts of findings have prompted Amazon to build servers next to those of partner companies in "co-location facilities" to cut down on latency (Farman 2018, 79). Minimizing delay is also crucial for content companies: A 2017 study concluded that after five seconds of buffering, 20 percent of people who started to watch the video would leave the service; after 10 seconds, half will be gone. After 20 seconds, only 30 percent would continue waiting (Farman 2017). As significant as these delays might be, they pale in comparison to the competitive world of algorithmic trading, where "low-latency trading" refers to systems and network routes used by financial institutions connecting to stock exchanges to rapidly execute financial transactions measured in milliseconds (Hasbrouck and Saar 2013). This led to the rise of high-frequency trading (HFT), where every additional millisecond might cost billions of dollars. Much like tech companies, hedge funds have been moving their server farms next to the stock exchange to gain competitive advantage –

changing the urban landscape of business capitals like New York.

The first and most common way in which both Silicon Valley and Wall Street use latency to maximize profit is therefore by introducing services or products that promise to limit its effect or eliminate it all together. Countless companies have promised their customers faster connectivity and improved loading speeds, from telecommunication giants like Verizon to Silicon Valley startups like Wix (a cloud-based web development platform). One such product is "Wix Turbo," launched in February 2019 via a high-profile campaign collaborating with Marvel Studios. In a one-minute ad featuring clips from Marvel's highly anticipated 2019 movie *Captain Marvel*, a male voice prods users to "stop blaming slow internet for your sluggish site" and, instead, pay for premium services offered by Wix to make sure their website will load faster. With over 12 million views on YouTube in less than a month, the Turbo Wix campaign was a successful attempt to bring together popular representations of speed, from superheroes to the "innovative technology" of data centers. With its emphasis on global infrastructure ("Wix now has 4x as many data centers worldwide"), this campaign illustrates the "infrastructuralization" of digital platforms (Plantin and Punathambekar 2019, 164).

A world without latency, however, is as fictional as the Marvel universe. While the promise of low latency is used to promote "premium services" or new products, a less understood way to commodify connectivity is by strategically introducing waiting and delay into gadgets and applications. Counterintuitively, "false latency" is a prevalent business model used by tech companies to establish trust or maximize profits (Farman 2018). This commodification of waiting takes different forms: it is part of Apple's annual launch of the latest version of its iPhone – a much-anticipated ritual involving news coverage of avid early adopters who camp outside Apple stores around the world. The images of endless lines and sleeping bags are ironic considering the fact that the very same company admitted to intentionally slowing down its iPhones (Gartenberg 2018). Another tech behemoth, Facebook, slowed down a "security check" feature to convince users that it is thorough and therefore trustworthy (Farman 2017). And tax-preparation software like TurboTax extends the wait time of users while it supposedly "maximizes" their refund. Slowness has also been commodified as part of a growing market of analog nostalgia: a mobile app named Gudak Cam, for instance, promises to reveal the photos taken by users only three days after they were shot, in an attempt to evoke the temporal aura and sense of wonderment attached to analog photography.

Alongside these examples, a recent testimony to the allure of built-in waiting can be found in Google's virtual assistant, which was announced at Google's Developers Conference, in California, in May 2018. In a keynote address that quickly went viral, Google's CEO Sundar Pichai boasts that the new robotic assistant is using a natural speech pattern that includes interjections such as "er" and "mmm-hmm" to make it sound more lifelike. Programmed to hesitate, wait, and murmur, this cutting-edge assistant is capable of placing phones calls, scheduling appointments, and ordering food while pretending to be human. This computational "failure" posits human imperfections such as hesitation or waiting as crucial for intimacy and trust. Google assistant's strategic "hmm..." was made to create the impression of uncertainty and by so doing recast it as human, all too human. Computers don't hesitate; they execute. By supposedly failing to execute a command as fast as possible and, instead, opting to pass time, Google's assistant succeeds in blurring the lines between bots and humans.

In other words, false latency is often a strategic way to create attachment to our machines. This complicates our understanding of techno-failure. Delay can be seen as failure only if it was not initially programmed. Once it is part of the code, a failure would be *the lack of delay*. Complete elimination of the digital murmur of voice assistants might render such devices less convincing to the unsuspecting human ear, and can therefore be seen as failure. This once again posits failure as both a judgment and a currency. It supports a business model that is rarely discussed, providing tech companies with various incentives to produce slowness, delay, and frustration.

The complex network of speed, regulation, and access has been foregrounded in recent debates regarding net neutrality and the myth of the "open internet." Much like latency-free infrastructure, the "open internet" is a cultural fantasy that has never been fully materialized. In practice, by 2017 the internet was controlled by several conglomerates functioning much like monopolies:

> Google, Facebook, Apple, Amazon, Netflix, and others manage access to most of the content created and delivered via broadband and wireless networks. Google appears to handle over 63 percent of searches, and it is projected to control 80 percent of the search ad market by 2019. Facebook exerts enormous control over access to news

online, and its unmanaged ad network appears to have torn democracy asunder. (Bogost 2017)

The net is not a "free and open" democracy; it is the playground (and goldmine) of an overly aggressive Big Tech industry.

The full elimination of net neutrality might lead to monopolization and lack of competition, as small companies will no longer be able to afford the access fees required by ISPs. It can also stifle free expression by favoring content produced by media conglomerates that are able to pay for "express lanes" (Ammori 2014). Still, the cultural fantasy of a "free internet," which Ian Bogost and others trace back to the counterculture and to the early days of network computing, never died. In recent years there have been numerous attempts to involve the general public in this complex and technical legislative issue (the most successful of which have been John Oliver's viral clips urging his viewers to pressure the Federal Communications Commission to save net neutrality).

Even when these decisions are made public, however, the exact nature of the deals between ISPs and content providers is revealed only if and when they reach the court of law. The complexity and opaqueness of crucial debates regarding the future of internet and telecommunication infrastructures was further illustrated in the recent introduction of 5G networks into the United States. Fifth generation (5G), the latest generation of cellular mobile communications, promises to reduce latency and enable massive device connectivity in the era of smart homes, smart cities, and the Internet of Things. On February 21, 2019, President Trump took to Twitter to voice his enthusiastic support of the new network: "I want 5G, and even 6G, technology in the United States as soon as possible. It is far more powerful, faster, and smarter than the current standard. American companies must step up their efforts, or get left behind. There is no reason that we should be lagging behind" (quoted in Mattern 2019). Yet, the introduction of 5G raises a host of concerns, among which are health anxieties surrounding the need for an additional 300,000 antennas across the United States and the lack of empirical research on long-term effects of radiofrequency electromagnetic radiation (CBS News 2018; Russell 2018). As anthropologist Shannon Mattern warned in her recent critique of 5G,

> The biggest concern is the fact that our technoutopian 5G fantasies (or what some scholars call "infrastructural imaginaries") – built atop a foundation of faster, smarter, stronger, and ubiquitous connectivity – are both fabricated and foiled by our infrastructural realities … In those remote and unprofitable markets unlikely ever to see fiber-optic cables or 5G cell towers, the *absence* of infrastructure gives lie to the dreams, long deferred, of universal, instantaneous connectivity. The 5G revolution, if it ever comes, will reach us unequally, re-instantiating geographies of uneven "progress." (Mattern 2019, original emphasis)

Mattern's analysis can help us push against a celebratory discourse casting 5G, in the words of Verizon CEO Hans Vestberg, as "the fourth industrial revolution" that promises "mobile speeds 100 times faster than that offered by our current 4G technology; and latency, or lag-time, cut to only a few milliseconds" (Mattern 2019). However, as 5G network requires building a dense network of cellular base stations and manufacturing (and buying) proprietary mobile devices, these promises have yet to materialize.

Moreover, its introduction in China created an arms race leading to rising tensions with the Trump administration. Citing security concerns, the United States has been pushing its allies to prevent Huawei, China's leading telecommunications producer, from building their next-generation computer and phone networks (Sanger et al. 2019). As the 5G example clearly demonstrates, any theorization of speed and enhanced connectivity must take into account political, global, and economic forces.

Failing to Remember: Buffering and Habitual New Media

If, as we argued above, latency is crucial to digital economies, why is it seldom discussed by users or media scholars? Digital dams such as servers, buffers, and limited bandwidth are constant reminders of the precarious nature of digital infrastructures, yet they are often denied and forgotten. A closer look at buffering can therefore help us map the mechanisms and contours of "habitual new media" (Chun 2016). As Chun proposes, habits are "things that remain by disappearing from consciousness" (2016, x). She traces the resurgence of habit in critical theory and media studies to the growing interest in the study of addiction: "Habit has moved from *habes* (to have) to *addictio* (to lose – to be forfeited to one's creditor). Habit is now a form of dependency, a condition of debt" (2016, 4). This, however, should not be mistaken for recasting habitual behaviors as inherently problematic or destructive. In fact, habit is essential for stability and creativity as it helps us minimize cognitive expenditures. Drawing on Bourdieu and Žižek, Chun reminds us that the question of habit is not solely psychological; it is, rather, "ideology in action" (2016, 7). It can be used to create a social equilibrium where members of the same class enjoy a "social harmony" that distinguishes them from others (Bourdieu 1977, 78). This intersection of psychology, biology, and ideology makes habit a productive entryway into the study of failure.

Unlike the Brechtian exposure of the fourth wall, which serves as an ideological and aesthetic device, buffering has become habitual and as such seems to be devoid of any real meaning or significance. Its recurrent occurrences are not emotionally moving or physically arousing; instead of the analog circulation of libido and pleasure described by Lucas Hilderbrand in his study of the VHS cassette and its "inherent vice" of degeneration (2009), users are often left gazing at the perpetual motion of the "loading" GIF while feeling helpless, isolated, and frustrated. Why, then, do most of them quickly forget and mostly trivialize their myriad encounters with the precarious nature of technology? We wish to offer several answers to the question of selective digital memory.

To begin with, buffering and the aesthetics of lag are often ignored due to the fact that they function within a larger framework of "web continuity." Traditionally, continuity is a term applied to the cinematic narrative. While cinema scholar David Bordwell (1985) studied how editing techniques create the illusion of continuity within the classical Hollywood film, buffering casts a

different light on the problem of fragmented spectatorship. Updating Bordwell's theory, Alexander Galloway
defines "web continuity" as "the set of techniques
practiced by webmasters that, taken as a totality, create
a pleasurable, fluid experience for the user" (2004,
65). The golden rule of "web continuity" is brilliantly
simple: Conceal the source. As Galloway writes, "In
classic Hollywood film, the apparatus is deliberately
removed from the image the same way that the process of production is removed from the commodity.
Although computers are very different, a similar logic
is at play" (2004, 65). Ironically, the constant need
not only to conceal the source but also to deny that
such a material source exists to begin with invokes an
affective response of anxiety and helplessness. The shift
from a seamless, continuous stream of moving images
to the endless loop of the "loading" GIF exposes the
digital infrastructure and destroys the illusion of web
continuity.

Still, while we might be momentarily frustrated
and anxious, the illusion of web continuity is quickly
restored as soon as the content streams once again. To
understand this dual process of acknowledgment and
denial, a short discussion of the ontology of habit is
in order. While Chun connects habit to the culture of
"upgrading" and constant crisis, for Elizabeth Grosz
habit "signals a milieu or environment that living beings
must internalize in order to live in comfort and with
minimal energy expenditure" (2013, 218). Building on
two French philosophers – Félix Ravaisson-Mollien and
Henri Bergson – Grosz argues that habit "produces a
state or a set of desires somewhere in between activity
and passivity, reversing and transforming the energies

of each toward a middle ground, a common milieu" (2013, 220).

This description is particularly productive for the study of buffering and its discontents. While the streaming revolution is based on the promise of seamless and on-demand access, buffering creates a phenomenological mode of waiting. Unlike the notorious commercial breaks on television – during which viewers can easily speculate how long the break will last and use the time to zap to another channel – the most disturbing aspect of buffering is *its unpredictable length*. We thus enter a liminal sphere of passivity and activity: automatically, we reach our hand to the mouse or to the touch screen, either to refresh the page or to fill the sudden void with something else. This reaction involves a choice between excessive activity and excessive passivity: On the one hand, we are restless, trying to use this suspended time to increase our productivity and atone for the sin of mindless binge-watching by cramming as many chores as possible (writing emails, checking the weather, making food). On the other hand, we are helpless to the point of paralysis. We might sit in our chair, gaze at the endless movement of the "loading" GIF, and pray that the buffering will eventually stop and that we can safely land, once again, in the immersive world of narrative and entertainment.

Being habitual, these actions *do not* produce new knowledge. As described by Grosz, "habit is the creation of a new bodily mode of existence, the learning of a way of simplifying action by selecting its key muscular efforts while hiding their conceptual accompaniments" (2013, 221). Our rooted assumptions regarding technology – the notion of a digital utopia that is always accessible and that caters to our individual needs – are thus maintained due to our habitual behavior. We might have waited for some time, but now we can hardly recall why, when, or for how long this liminal mode of experience has lasted.

This once again connects buffering to the cognitive function of human memory. Daniel Kahneman famously demonstrated that there exists an important distinction between our "experiencing self" and our "remembering self". While the first lasts about three seconds and vanishes without a trace, the latter consists of changes in the story, significant moments in the story, and the way the story ends (Kahneman and Riis 2005). This behavioral theory is crucial to the study of buffering – a temporary lag that mostly ends with the return to seamless streaming. Once it ends, our "remembering self" tends to push it aside – creating the "cognitive illusion" that it never took place. Based on a series of studies, Kahneman and Jason Riis concluded that our remembering self is "prone to error" (2005, 285), which might explain why most users will find it almost impossible to accurately report *when* they encountered buffering and *how long* it lasted. Researching how humans remember physical pain or listen to a symphony, they assert that the brain has a "negativity bias" that hard-wires us to remember intense and negative experiences more than positive ones (Kahneman and Riis 2005, 286). While buffering can be described as a negative experience, its initial intensity has been eliminated due to its habitual function and, mostly, "happy ending."

Following this line of thought, we wish to argue that buffering remains habitual and therefore prevents new knowledge on the machine to emerge onto the surface.

Yet, the fact that buffering has become habitual does not mean that it no longer produces any response. In fact, our encounter with buffering is being experienced on three different levels: as temporary emotional distress; as a disruption that triggers various bodily reactions (touching the screen, leaving our comfortable seat, clicking the mouse, etc.); and as an enduring and unrecognized affective response of "perpetual anxiety" (Alexander 2017).

Returning to our discussion of Sara Ahmed's "affective economies" in chapter 1, we argue that failure functions as an affective economy when the idea it might reveal is instantaneously replaced with another, less threatening idea. And so buffering might be attached to a reassuring idea like "I forgot to reconnect the router" and/or "this temporary disturbance will soon end." What remains concealed is the idea that buffering induces a "perpetual anxiety" which, in turn, reveals a structure of meaning to our world: the fact that we increasingly rely on machines and infrastructures that unpredictably work or don't work properly. Recasting buffering as a technical, soon-to-disappear nuisance therefore involves the very same system of "difference and displacement" described by Ahmed.

Functioning as part of the neoliberal promise machine described in chapter 1, buffering is a remarkable example of the delayed promise of seamlessness. Silicon Valley has been able to convince internet users in Western countries that they are entitled to seamless access to the digital ecosystem by promoting a blind faith in compression and automation. But the promise to provide infinite connectivity around the world is yet to be materialized, and hence it is repeatedly delayed.

Conclusion

Buffering is a useful entryway into various concerns surrounding our ever-growing dependency on internet connectivity: the new "economy of access" based on the digital divide between geographical areas, national borders, and "standard" and "premium" services; the loss of communal viewing experiences due to the emergence of an individualized, habitual consumption of online content; and, finally, the production of an affective economy based on anxiety, helplessness, and the constant denial of the "unknowable" nature of both our technology and our world.

Still, digital noise is sometimes experienced as pleasurable rather than anxiety-inducing. This is because waiting plays an important role in the production of intimacy and attachment. Anticipation is often associated with hope, excitement, and imagination. It can provide sought-after opportunities for reflection, or it can open up a space for emotional and cognitive contemplation.

This duality helps us understand why habitual failure *does not* make a difference. Within our constantly changing habitual behavior, it does not create new knowledge of either our world or our tools. The denial of buffering is therefore triadic: first, it is forgotten due to new habitual patterns shaped by the growing dependency on digital technology and mobile devices; second, it is systematically downplayed as part of a broader discourse of "solutionism" and "technological fetishism" (Tierney 1993; Morozov 2013); and third, it functions as a delayed promise of seamlessness, where the fact that the fulfillment of the promise is repeatedly impeded serves, paradoxically, to reinforce the attachment to digital devices and faster networks.

This delayed promise supports a system of inequality and information asymmetry in a manner similar to that of the derivative form, which will be studied in the next chapter. To push against the myths of immateriality and seamless connectivity, we must turn our gaze to those daily, habitual failures that we encounter like "raisins in a pudding" (Nakamura 2009, 87): Everywhere, always – but never at the same time.

Chapter 4
Too Big to Fail: Banks, Derivatives, and Market Collapse

Introduction

If buffering is an example of habitual failure, of that type of failure that doesn't make a difference, a short analysis of the financial collapse of 2007–8 can help us ask what happens when failure leaves the habitual realm and makes a devastating, real impact on the lives of millions. This chapter will therefore offer detailed examples of how "the promise machine" works to connect anxiety, uncertainty, and ignorance, and thus habituates us to seeing systemic failures as a responsibility that ordinary citizens must share with the big financial players.

Both habitual debt production and the habitual forgetting of the anxieties and frustrations of buffering reflect a common corporate reliance on teaching users to forget downturns because they will always – and eventually – give way to upturns, exemplified by better streaming experiences, more goods and services acquired through debt, fewer bankruptcies, fewer total software breakdowns, and greater prospects of a smoother path from anxiety to happiness in streaming and in personal finance. In both cases, forgetting the unpleasant (temporary) past is the key to a seamless future of entertainment, information, or greater buying power. This is what both financial and digital corporations specialize in, so that the past failure, however traumatic, is rendered forgettable and the future success is promised to be eternal and continuous. Debt in the relationship of ordinary users of credit cards, takers of loans, and holders of mortgages and insurance policies could be seen as a sort of buffered financial experience, in which we are taught to regularly forget the trauma of waiting, interruption, billing cycles, and credit decision delays. In this chapter, we draw on previous work by Appadurai (2016), which also engages the growing body of work by sociologists and anthropologists on contemporary finance, but we also note that our argument here, both in its effort to thematize failure and in its effort to connect Wall Street and Silicon Valley, does not have any noteworthy conceptual predecessors.

To better understand how this reliance on debt is being produced and exploited by Wall Street, a closer look at the 2008 market collapse is in order. The financial markets depend on three kinds of failure, which are nested in one another. The first is the most colloquial sense of failure that became a part of the public vocabulary in the financial collapse of 2007–8, which was quickly categorized as a classic example of market failure. The second sort of failure is our failure to see that, as ordinary citizens, we had largely failed to understand the black box of financial markets, and had allowed ourselves, as savers, debtors, and investors, to remain structurally ignorant of how profits are actually made in financial markets. The third failure, which is the most insidious part of the workings of derivatives markets, consists of the failed promises, whose accumulation and scale are the key to the mortgage crisis of 2007–8. The systemic weakness of the larger financial system within which derivatives circulate is that it allows for the *repeated commoditization of prior promises by new promises*, thus diluting and disseminating the force of the promise across many players (traders) who bear only tiny portions of the burden of the larger interlinked system of promises that comprises the overall value of any particular derivatives market. This opens the systemic possibility of failure, breakdown, and collapse even when the bulk of individual trades meet their local conditions of felicity. In this perspective, the three types of failure converge in explaining the crisis of 2007–8, since they inform and underwrite one another.

The Derivative Form

We argue in this chapter that financialized capitalism (the monetization of financial risks to create new and endlessly derivative forms of profit), is a deeply unequal system that relies on the strategic and mostly under-studied distribution of failure. The instruments and institutions of global finance assure that the financial elite builds its profits on the debt accumulation of the majority and, at the same time, when its own activities fail on a massive scale, they rely on the assets of ordinary tax payers to deflect this failure, and make the persistent argument that their own institutions are "too big to fail." How is this radical shift of responsibility accomplished? What ties together debt, derivatives, and failure?

The argument of an earlier book on financial derivatives by one of us was that the failure of the financial system in 2007–8 in the United States was primarily a failure of language (Appadurai 2015). This argument does not deny that greed, ignorance, weak regulation, and irresponsible risk-taking were important factors in the collapse. But the new role of language in the marketplace is the condition of possibility for all these more easily identifiable flaws.

To make this case requires understanding how language takes on a new life in contemporary finance, and this argument takes us into a realm not usually explored when financial markets are discussed. To understand how language takes on the role it does in finance today, four steps are involved. The first is to show how derivatives are the core technical innovation that characterizes contemporary finance. The second step is to show how derivatives are, essentially, written contracts about the future prices of various types of financial assets, the essence of which are promises by the losing party to pay the winning party an agreed sum of money, in the event of a specific future price outcome. Thus, the contract is a promise, and to understand it fully requires a new look at contracts, seen as promises about the uncertain future. This requires a rereading of J.L. Austin's (1975) work on performatives and their conditions of felicity. Returning to our definition of the "Austinian promise" in chapter 1, this analysis of derivative contracts brings out the special importance of language in the financial marketplace. The third step is to show how the derivative form exploits the linguistic power of the contract through the special form that money takes in the financial world, given that money is by definition the most abstract form in which the value of commodities can be expressed. The fourth and final step is to understand that the failure of the derivatives market (especially in the domain of housing mortgages) is primarily about failed promises (promises are the most important in Austin's typology of performatives), a type of failure that was neither occasional nor ad hoc but that became systematic and contagious, thus bringing the entire financial market to the brink of disaster. This focus on failed promises was already signaled in our Introduction, and we explored it in relation to technology in chapter 3.

Our current era of financialization is without precedent in the speed and scope of the innovations that have characterized it. Financialization may be broadly defined as the process that permits money to be used to make more money through the use of instruments that exploit the role of money in credit, speculation, and investment. Its deep historical roots lie in the epoch of expanded maritime trade and in the growth of the idea of hazard insurance for those merchants who traded their goods across large oceanic distances during this period. Though this early period was still preoccupied by the divine and natural hazards that beset maritime commerce, the emergence of actuarial thinking at this time was the first effort to bring secular control to the likelihood of disaster at sea, and insurers began to offer means of protection to merchants who feared the loss of their goods in transit. The reasoning behind this early actuarial history was a mixture of theological and statistical perceptions of risk, and it constitutes the first effort to distinguish statistically calculable risk from divine and natural uncertainty, a distinction that is the very foundation of modern finance.

The next big shift that is critical to the current power of finance is to be found in the commodity markets, notably in Chicago, in which traders first began to traffic in what became "futures," first in agrarian commodities (such as wheat and pork bellies) and then, gradually, to "futures" trades in all commodities with any significant market with unpredictable fluctuations in prices. Terms such as "put" and "call," "option" and "hedge" can be dated to these futures markets of the mid-nineteenth century, which remain important today, though to a lesser degree than in the period of their birth. In these futures markets, there was the first move toward separating the market in future prices from the market in current prices for commodities. These commodity futures are the earliest form of financial "assets," which are now distinguishable from the actual commodities whose prices underlie them. Today's derivatives (this term referring to the fact that future commodities are derivable from current commodities) are an extraordinary extension of these early futures contracts.

The link between the early history of insurance and the early history of futures markets is that any risk of a positive change in prices (what we today call upside risks), about which a trader has doubts, can be offset, or in effect can be insured against, by taking a "hedge" position that protects traders who are convinced of a downside risk for the particular commodity price in a specific time horizon. The hedge is essentially a dynamic form of insurance.

What the derivative is and what it does are closely tied. The derivative is an asset whose value is based on that of another asset, which could itself be a derivative. In a chain of links that contemporary finance has made indefinitely long, the derivative is above all a linguistic phenomenon, since it is primarily a referent to something more tangible than itself: it is a proposition or a belief about another object that itself might be similarly derived from yet another similar object. Since the references and associations that compose a derivative chain have no status other than the credibility of their reference to something more tangible than themselves, the derivative's claim to value is essentially linguistic, though not for that reason less real in its systemic effects. Furthermore, its force is primarily performative, and it is primarily tied up with context, convention, and felicity. More specifically still, while the derivative is thus a linguistic artifact, it is even more specific in that it is an invitation to a performative insofar as derivatives take full force when they are traded – that is, when two traders arrive at a written contract to exchange (buy and sell) a specific bundle of derivatives. The promise is for one of them to pay money to the other depending on who proves to be right about the future price (after a particular and specified temporal term) of that specific derivative. In this sense, of course, all contracts have a promissory element (Fried 1981). But the derivative form is the sole contractual form that is based on the unknown future value of an asset traded between two persons. Other contracts have known future values, known terms, and known current values (such as with loans, rents, and other pecuniary contracts). Thus, when an entire market driven by derivatives comes to the edge of collapse, there must be a deep underlying flaw in the linguistic world that derivatives presuppose.

The Derivative Promise

The link between derivatives and language turns on the question of promises, which we view, following Austin, as one class of performatives, or linguistic utterances that, if produced under the right conditions, create the conditions of their own truth. Elie Ayache, a derivatives trader and a French social thinker, has established the importance of seeing derivatives as written contracts (Ayache 2010). We are indebted to him for establishing that derivatives, in the end, break free of the prison of probability and that specific derivative trades, in real-time conditions, are best seen as written contracts. Ayache's analysis shows that real-life derivative trading is not about using probabilistic or statistical methods to predict trends in prices, but is a much more contingent, context-sensitive, and qualitative process through which traders set prices for objects whose future value is both unknown and highly subject to volatility.

Today's derivative contracts, like all modern contracts, are, ideally, in written form, and their underlying force comes from the fact that they are composed of a mutual pair of promises: a promise to pay in one direction or another, at the expiry of a fixed period of time, and depending on the price of the derivative at that future time. This mutually binding promise is initially oral and only incidentally committed to writing as confirmation and for the purposes of tracking and record-keeping. A derivative trade is complete when the two traders, often on the phone, say, "It's done"

(Wosnitzer 2014). This is a classic Austinian performative moment.

In Austinian terms, the conditions of felicity for this pair of promises to take force include the mutual knowledge of the traders; the capacity of their larger institutions to fulfill the downside risk of large payments; and the general social network of managers, regulators, small shareholders, and large investors, which lend an appropriate audience (even if virtual) for the transaction. These actors collaborate in the systemic dissemination of contractual promises, in a manner that has been described as a performative chain (Appadurai 2015). Put another way, when the contractual nature of the promise is subject to infinite further monetization, risks can be taken on prior risks and money can be made using speculative instruments that involve growing distances between derivatives and their underlying assets, which are frequently themselves derivative. This recursive chain of derivatives is the essence of the world of the subprime housing mortgage.

As long as housing values continued to rise (and seemed likely to rise indefinitely), the growth of the market in housing derivatives, composed of a huge chain of derivative trades, based on bundling individual mortgages, seemed to be built on a reasonably positive relationship between the value of homes and the value of housing derivatives, which could sustain an exponentially growing derivative market. In other words, the ratio of housing values to the value of derivatives based on mortgages could be seen as systemic protection against collective risk. But the housing market, as it had to eventually, did collapse, and the ability of various sellers of housing derivatives to find buyers disappeared, creating a freezing of liquidity and a grinding stop for the promise machine.

Each promise made in the great chain of promises represented by the trade in housing derivatives was reasonably valid. But the capacity of the overall system to bear the load of the chain of promises was stressed beyond easy retrieval. This disjuncture has partly to do with the volume of promises creating immense cross-cutting promissory chains that were bound to weaken as they became more extended. Worse, every link in the promissory chain was built on greater risk, as the distance from the underlying asset was increased. The greater the distance between the two, the larger the gap between the real value of the underlying stock of homes and the overall derivative system based on housing. In the mortgage market of recent years in the United States, traders sought to move their toxic derivatives rapidly to the next buyer, as the inevitable drop in housing values became more imminent. At the end of this chain was the insurance giant AIG, which in effect was caught holding a massive number of toxic derivatives when the music stopped in 2007.

The conventional wisdom, reiterated in the popular media, and in numerous books and articles by industry insiders, regulators, analysts, and academics, tends to place the blame for the collapse on irresponsible lenders, greedy traders, co-opted rating agencies, and weak regulations. Each of these has some relevance. But at the heart of the collapse of the housing derivatives market – and thus of the financial markets as a whole – was the form of the derivative, which involves piling risk on risk, thus making risk an independent source of profit, with little basis in the realities of production, price, and commodity flows. In a world of derivative assets, money breeds more money, if risks can be bought and sold through securitization, the process by which debts can be bundled, repackaged, and sold, time and again. This dynamic liberates money almost entirely from Marx's famous M-C-M formula and allows money to grow, as if magically, on its own, through risk-based credit trading. Understanding this development requires a fresh look at the money form, historically the most abstract way in which human beings have reckoned both with value and with price. In the case of Silicon Valley, discussed in the previous chapters, this sense that money can breed money, without much need for any major change in production and manufacturing technologies, is reflected in the mammoth investments made in promising Silicon Valley startups, the extraordinary prices paid when these startups are bought by other entrepreneurs, and the astronomical valuations of their future potential and possible profits. Of course, as we have noted already, this does not make Silicon Valley and Wall Street identical in their modes of delinking price from value, as startup investments and technological unicorns work differently from mortgage bundling, asset-backed securities and other complex derivative instruments. Nevertheless, both forms of monetizing reflect their shared faith in the calculability of financial assets in the future.

This supports an economy of waiting, which we already studied in chapter 3. In fact, waiting is the key link between the two experiences of techno-failure and market failure: waiting for credit approvals, waiting for the gap between receiving loans and paying interest on them, or waiting for the reloading to be complete.

Waiting and queuing are widely known to be conditions of subordination and inequality (Tawil-Souri 2017). So, too, with Wall Street and Silicon Valley, we are trained, as viewers and debtors, to wait for the next moment of gratification, and we are also trained to forgive and forget the endless recurrence of traumatic buffering periods. Within the economy of risk, waiting is much more than being bored and passing time; the combination of waiting and anxiety can coerce subjects into making desperate decisions or living in a perpetual "survival mode," which leaves them more vulnerable to various forms of exploitation.

We have noted that this independence from the movement of prices is already presaged in the commodity futures markets of the mid-nineteenth century, when it became possible to make wagers on future commodity prices without ever acquiring or using the commodities in which trade was occurring. What the contemporary derivative form accomplishes is to make this wager on future prices indifferent to individual risk preferences, to price volatility, and even to the prior history of prices for the asset in question. This is the point at which the heart of the derivative form reveals itself to be a virtually pure linguistic phenomenon, which we already defined as an *agonistic promise*, a promise to pay the other party if the other party is wrong and you prove to be right about a future commodity price.

As stated in the Introduction, an agonistic promise, unlike the pure Austinian promise, requires two parties whose promises to pay one another have to be simultaneous and mutually exclusive, so that both promises (which together compose the derivatives contract) meet the same conditions of felicity, though only one of them can be profit-making at the end of the stipulated period of the contract. The second key feature of this sort of agonistic promise is that it depends on the endless tradability of any particular bundle of assets (such bundles are often called securities), something that resembles the endless circulability of money. Failure – or collapse – occurs when the system-wide relations between the buyers and sellers of these assets (measurable by the total dollar value of the derivatives market at any point in time) enter into a crisis because there are no buyers for large amounts of these instruments. This thus creates a monumental pile of debt without another buyer left to pick up the mountain of risk now accumulated in the derivatives market.

This is the point in 2008 when the state was forced to come in and buy large numbers of these toxic instruments in order to artificially jump-start the financial markets by producing liquidity from its own coffers when no one else was willing or able to do so. At this point, the accelerating and growing chain of performatives ("promises") can grow no further. No one can meet the felicity conditions to make even more agonistic promises, and the situation threatens to collapse on itself, or move backward and downward, exposing the fragility of many of the promises previously made in the building up of this chain. Put another way, what collapsed in 2007–8 was a house of words made of contracts, each contract consisting of an agonistic pair of promises, together composing a performative chain as well as a performative mountain generated by the accrual of money value by the multiplication of wagers on uncertain future prices. When the markets froze – when no buyers could be found for any serious bundle of derivatives – what collapsed was the architecture of promises on which financial profits are composed in the age of the derivative form. In Silicon Valley, both in the last decade and in the earlier dot.com bubble, the key to speculative risk-taking, primarily by startup financiers, is the bet on new technologies, usually not in their material or physical possibilities, but in their potential to attract large numbers of fee-paying users or massive advertising revenues. In the case of Wall Street, the promise machine is eventually about future prices for derivative assets, whereas in the case of Silicon Valley the wager is on the potential of any new technology to attract either huge numbers of end users or relatively small numbers of paying subscribers.

Debt and Market Failure

In chapter 3, we demonstrated how tech companies could monetize latency and waiting. A similar argument could be made regarding Wall Street. Failure, we argue, has been transformed by Wall Street into a commodity by way of debt production. Just as buffering paradoxically strengthens our attachments to our machines, market failures sustain our "wounded attachments" to capitalist logics and to constant states of crisis alike (Brown 1995).

We have recently come to see that one primary threat to international order is the volatility of global financial markets. Capitalism today surrounds and saturates us in a way it never did before. In its home regions, notably in the United States, it has taken the form of deep financialization. Finance now far exceeds the sphere of production and manufacture of industrial goods. Since the early 1970s we have had the rapid development of a host of financial instruments, most importantly the derivative, which were barely imaginable in the time of Karl Marx. The breakthrough that made this financial explosion possible was the idea that risk itself could be monetized, allowing a small set of actors to take risks on risks. This is the core of the logic of the derivative, an instrument that has allowed financial technicians and managers to make virtually every part of our everyday lives susceptible to monetization. In this way, housing has now been turned into a machine for monetizing mortgages; the environment has been monetized through carbon trading and many other derivatives; education has been captured through sophisticated methods of creating student debt; health and insurance have been thoroughly penetrated by models of risk, arbitrage, and bets on the future. In short, everyday life is linked to capital not so much by the mechanism of the surplus value of labor but through making us all risk-bearers, whose aggregate risk can be endlessly combined and recombined to provide new forms of risk-taking and profit-making by the financial industries. Failure is a meta-commodity whose value is constantly reinforced. By this we mean that while derivatives create an indefinite distance between commodities (of the traditional sort) and financial assets, failure emerges as a sort of meta-commodity which also creates value, not by utility, demand, and supply, but by guaranteeing that ordinary debtors remain believers in the debt–credit machinery even when it fails them repeatedly. We are all laborers now, regardless of what we do, insofar as our primary reason for being is to enter into debt and thus be forced to monetize the risks of health, security, education, housing, and much else in our lives. This labor of debt production is inconceivable without the normalization of failure, and that too at several levels. First, we have to assume and absorb our regular failure to live within our means and thus to view debt as a natural fact. Second, we have to accept that some of us will go bankrupt and that this is an acceptable outcome in the bigger scheme of things. Third, in the order of things, we learn to accept that some banks, hedge funds, and financial schemes will also fail and with them the dreams and hopes of those who invested in them. And finally, we learn to accept that the risk and the lived experience of failure constitute the price of entry into an inevitably deferred state of wealth, security, and happiness.

However, the global spread of the capitalist imaginary has by no means been arrested or compromised. Banks, hedge funds, and insurance companies are aggressively pushing their way into new markets, seeking to lobby for legislation that will allow them to bring the same untrammeled debt markets from which they profited (and which also crashed in 2008) to the countries of the Global South. Thus, it is only a matter of time before the countries of the Global South also find themselves fully exposed to the volatility, inscrutability, and extra-legality of the derivative-based financial markets of the North. As James Baldwin once said in another context, "no more water, the fire next time." To better understand this dangerous process, let us recall some relevant Marxist ideas.

Marx's central insight about the workings of industrial capitalism was (in the three volumes of *Capital*, 1887) to notice the distinction between absolute and relative surplus value. In simple terms, absolute surplus value was to be found in increasing the amount of labor that a firm could apply to producing commodities for sale, as by increasing the number of workers or by increasing the length of the workday. Relative surplus value, on the other hand, was generated by improvements in technology, workplace organization, or other means by which labor productivity could be increased without hiring more workers or paying for more labor time. This is how a given firm could compete with other firms that were producing the same commodity. The key to the appropriation of relative surplus value was to make a given amount of labor produce more profit, without increasing wages. The difference was profit in the hands of the capitalist.

Today's financial capitalism, which Marx could not have entirely foreseen in his day, does not primarily work through the making of profit in the commodity sphere, though a certain part of the capitalist economy still operates in this sphere. By far the larger portion works by making profit on the monetization of risk, and risk is made available to the financial markets through debt in its myriad forms. All of us who live in a financialized economy generate debt in many forms: consumer debt, housing debt, health debt, and others related to these. Capitalist forms also operate through debt (since borrowing on the capital markets has become much more important for large corporations than issuing stock or "equity").

From this it follows that the key to transforming the current form of financial capitalism is to seize and appropriate the means of the production of debt, in the interest of the vast class of debt producers, rather than the small class of debt manipulators. It is not debt as such that is bad, since it allows us to bring future value into the present. The challenge, rather, is to socialize and democratize the profit produced by the monetization of debt, so that those of us who actually produce debt can also be the main beneficiaries of its monetization.

But the problem of debt is that those who produce exploitable debt value as their labor are local, while financial markets, networks, and corporations are global. Put another way: *all debt is local, but all debt markets are global.* By expanding this aphorism, we can return to a deeper understanding of the slogan that some banks are "too big to fail."

The notion that the big banks responsible for the mortgage collapse of 2007–8 were too big to fail also raises the question of temporality and of the staging of emergency in the dominant financial discourses of our times. The big banks are often argued to be in need of being broken up or reorganized, by voices both within and outside the financial industries, but *not yet, not now.* This is a particularly painful paradox because it is in the moment of crisis that banks reveal their greed for profit, their willingness to take risks with other people's money, their indifference to regulation, and their bottomless belief in the importance of what they do for capitalism as a whole. And yet this is the very moment in which they are able to argue that they cannot be reformed, restricted, or regulated, because that would lead us over the edge, into the abyss of darkness from which there is no possible return.

Thus, the "now" of regulation and reform is deferred into a perpetual "later," and later never comes, because the habitual cycle of debt, interest, risk, profit, and failed promises re-establishes itself, after a little bloodletting of weak banks and some mild punishment of the greediest corporate actors. Indeed, the promise machine of the derivative-centered market has been more or less fully restored since 2008, and a decade later the biggest banks, hedge funds, and mega-investors are making more obscene profits than ever.

The idea that some of the biggest banks responsible for putting the United States economy at risk of collapse in 2007–8 were "too big to fail" was rooted in the circular reasoning in which bank-generated credit was the fuel of advanced capitalism and the corollary that any effort to dismantle or break up these banks would compromise the flow of this life-sustaining substance. This view, promoted by the biggest banks and echoed by regulators, politicians, and policy-makers, led to a massive redirection of public money into saving these banks, notably in the program called TARP (Troubled Asset Relief Program) in the US and the EFSF (European Financial Stability Facility) in the EU, but also through other devices. This series of bailouts assured the survival of these banks in 2008, and more or less guaranteed the continuation and expansion of their risky practices into the present and the foreseeable future.

There is a direct link between consumer debt (gen erated through credit cards, auto loans, housing mortgages, student loans, insurance, and policies) and the global market in derivatives. Here we cannot avoid some large numbers: The total global debt in January 2018 was $233 trillion, of which $68 trillion was composed of debts held by non-financial corporations, $63 trillion was held by governments, $58 trillion was held by financial institutions, and household debt was $44 trillion (Chu 2018).

Let us put these very large numbers in plain language. The household debt in the world (consumer debt, household loans of every type, mortgages, insurance, etc.) appears to be about 12 percent of the world's total debt. But this number is a bit misleading, since governments, business corporations, and financial institutions also depend on investments and payments from the general public (as tax payers, shareholders, bond holders, and investors, small and large). In this sense, all debt is consumer debt. But let us concede that 12 percent of the world's debt is directly produced by consumer borrowing and the rest by indirect extraction from consumers of every degree of wealth.

All derivatives are based on debt, of one variety or another. We can then begin to see how to connect the dots between debts, derivatives, and big banks. An excellent guide to this connection is to be found in a 2016 piece by a respected analyst from the American corporate world:

> Unlike standard loans and stock investments that actually help grow an economy, derivatives are a zero-sum game. It is exactly like playing in a casino, one must lose for someone else to win. *Derivatives are a wealth-transfer tool from the uninformed, unsuspecting investor, saver, or retiree to informed market insiders.* So, even if banks can avoid losses on derivative bets, investors still get hit.
>
> Derivatives explain why so many Americans lost value in their homes, retirement accounts, and life savings after the 2008–09 crash. The news media reported that more than $5 trillion disappeared from the market in that downturn. But the money did not just disappear – that would be against the law of physics. It only got transferred from

the masses to the few. If this happens again, extreme civic unrest could damage global financial markets for a long time. When the potential damage can be so large, some regulation is needed to protect Main Street from the massive gambling instruments of Wall Street. (Jones 2016, emphasis added)

This cogent analysis spells out the relationship between our guaranteed failure as debtors and the guaranteed successes of the "few." It also draws our attention to the information asymmetry that informs our relation both to financial markets and to "black-box" technologies. "Too big to fail" can be better translated into the proposition that no one is too small to fail, as debtors will likely see their personal economy crash (unpayable consumer loans, burdensome student loans, unaffordable insurance policies, ballooning second mortgages, bankrupted pension funds) so that the major financial players, in banks, pension funds, and other hugely leveraged financial institutions can remain "too big to fail." Thus, in the financial markets, the ordinary citizen, the quotidian producer of debt value, is systemically doomed to be exploited by the tiny financial elite. This is a *guaranteed failure*, whose continued reproduction is routinely re-presented as the main condition of the success of the global financial market.

Conclusion

We began this chapter with the argument that the underlying cause of the financial crisis of 2007–8 was the mortgage meltdown, which was, in turn, based on the collapse of the failed promises represented by the derivatives market. We then went on to argue that the form of production whose value is expropriated and exploited by the financial elites is debt production by consumers. This consumer debt production undergirds the mega-debts of states, banks, and other corporations. The key point of linkage is that the success of the derivatives market relies on the regular upward flow of consumer debt, and when this performative chain – this chain of promises – fails, as it eventually must, the consumer, as tax payer, is called upon to reassure those who *cannot* fail (because they are too big) that they will not, in fact, fail, and that the cost of their failures is pushed to the bottom of the chain, to tax payers and consumers, resulting in delinquent credit payments, bankrupt mortgages, and vanishing mortgages. It is this very consumer debtor who is transmuted into the perennial beta-tester of Silicon Valley, discussed in chapter 2, where obsolescence and innovation were shown to be the twin drivers of technological change.

Market failure is often treated as an inevitable and infrequent result of excessive speculation, inadequate regulation, or unscrupulous bankers. It is rarely seen as a systemic feature of the connection of markets to wider aspects of our social and technological lives under advanced capitalism. The habitual failures involved in consumer debt (such as dubious loans, inadequate payments, and the longing for more and new goods) are the very basis for those gigantic global risk markets, in which the promise machine transforms our little risks into the outsize risks of the financial industries. What is more, the large financial players usually win, and ordinary consumers usually lose, and the crucial ideological lesson that we are forced to accept is that such massive collapses are the fundamental precondition of our own financial security. This false lesson is daily reinforced by the tools, slogans, and campaigns of the information economy, and its protocols of sharing, streaming, and buffering. These protocols, both obscure and routine, have become the major stage on which the disguise of systemic failure and its projection onto the end user is enacted.

Conclusion: Failure, Remembered

The specters haunting our discussion of failure are many. As Wall Street and Silicon Valley have been controlling and shaping the conditions under which failure has been either remembered or ignored, users are faced with habitual failure, whose existence is constantly denied. This brings failure closer to the idea of erasure. Banks are "too big to fail," yet debt incurred by students or patients is very rarely erased or forgiven.

Think, for example, of the multiple meanings of the word "savings": it once stood for the culmination of a life's work, the ability to function as a responsible, productive citizen whose fortune could provide a safety net for both herself and her family members. It implies both the recognition that human existence involves uncertainty and contingency (hence the need to save for a rainy day) and an inherent, unshakable trust in the financial system. The money is safe in the bank, where it can earn interest and, if nothing else, retain its value.

This, however, is no longer true. Today we can also read "savings" as the saving of data or information that might be used against us – the ability to monitor and save everything we do online and offline. The failure to erase, or to forgive someone for a bad decision or a one-time mistake, creates a culture in which some, yet not all, are being perpetually punished for their failures. This, once again, reminds us that failure is a privilege: (some) men can "fail up," while women almost always fail down (having their images circulate forever as a form of "revenge porn," losing their jobs, or being held accountable for their mistakes as well as for the mistakes of others).

In theory, one easy solution to the kind of failures studied in this book – from techno-failure to market failure – is opting out: not using apps or digital services, or staying out of the stock market. This raises the difficult question of choice and consent, which was implied throughout the book but has not been addressed directly. The notion of active participation – the fact that the user voluntarily chooses to subscribe to a digital platform or app after (not) reading the strategically convoluted "terms of use" – is useful in describing why algorithmic systems are growing ever more ubiquitous. In *Obfuscation: A User's Guide for Privacy and Protest* (2015), Finn Brunton and Helen Nissenbaum criticize "the fantasy of opting out" by claiming that while the algorithmic systems tracking our behavior are voluntary, they constitute "asymmetrical relationships" (2015, 55). "Opting out" of digital connectedness is therefore "increasingly unreasonable" (2015, 54). Focusing on a company like Netflix, for example, can serve to remind us that "opting out" is also a class privilege: with the demise of local video stores, domestic "cine-clubs," and automated DVD rental kiosks, the ability to watch a variety of films and television shows without paying for an expensive cable subscription is limited. If one does not live in a coastal city like New York or L.A. – with their art-house cinemas, film festivals, and numerous media libraries – it is otherwise impossible to gain access to unlimited content for less than $10 per month (the price of a Netflix subscription fee).

This question of avoidance or resistance becomes ever more complex once we return to the notion that "technology *disappears* into the human world" (Jarzombek 2016, 5, original emphasis). As we asked in chapter 1, is not the failure of the smartphone simply the failure of the iron hammer as the wooden handle breaks? The answer is "no," as habitual failure in the age of digital and financial markets holds unique patterns. Without the ability to easily distinguish Man from Tool, our failed technologies and markets do not teach us something new about our world; their repeated breakdowns do nothing more than further obstruct the underlying logic and hidden infrastructures that sustain them. At the same time, these failures are being commodified, studied, and fed into the perpetual cycle of feedback and testing. While blaming ourselves for misuse or recklessness, we teach machine-learning algorithms how to become more successful in predicting our future behaviors. In short, the routinization of failure has become a primary condition for the boundlessly creative destruction of contemporary capitalism.

The same could be said about the highly complex and manipulative system of debt production. One of the many challenges we now face is how to resist the sense that the global process of debt production is inevitable and that it cannot be subverted. The question is: What sort of politics needs to be produced to resist it? The main answer that has emerged in various parts of the world is debt refusal, as in important segments of the "Occupy" movement (Graeber 2011). Debt refusal by mortgage owners, students, pension-holders, and others certainly is a legitimate political tactic, insofar as it offers an immediate tool for starving the beast of financial capitalism. But is it enough? Is it even the best way of making capitalism work for the 99 percent?

For one, debt refusal is not accessible to those who cannot afford basic necessities such as food, shelter, and medical insurance. As this mode of resistance is therefore limited in its scope, we doubt that it can propagate the kind of structural changes needed to break the promise machine and its reliance on the monetization of failure.

From this, it follows that the key to transforming the current form of financial capitalism is to seize and appropriate the means of the production of debt, in the interest of the vast class of debt producers, rather than the small class of debt manipulators. It is not debt as such that is bad, since it allows us to bring future value into the present. The challenge, rather, is to socialize and democratize the profit produced by monetization of debt, so that those of us who actually produce debt can also be the main beneficiaries of its monetization. However, as chapter 4 demonstrated, the problem of debt is that those who produce exploitable debt value as their labor are local, while global financial markets, networks, and corporations are global. From this perspective, the local always loses. This argument about debt converges with recent arguments about the centrality of debt to contemporary capitalism (Lazzarato 2012).

Instead of choosing among these weak alternatives, we wish to end this study of habitual failure with a provocation, a call to limit our possibilities rather than expand them. What we need to resist is not just buying the newest iPhone or investing in the latest derivative form, but rather the promise of convenience as a reliable product of endless choice. The illusion of choice is the oil that connects Wall Street and Silicon Valley, two cultural worlds that market scarce resources as if they were infinite. The most radical resistance might therefore be to develop a cultural and economic climate in which consumers are faced with a limited number of choices. This can open up ways to help consumers compare different products, study them, and care for them for longer periods of time.

The supposed freedom to choose is also what creates the very real sense of exhaustion and lethargy described in chapter 1. Financial and technological failures, even while being ignored, produce a set of demands that can lead to the demise of biological and cognitive functions. In that sense, they do make a difference – albeit this sensory endurance is seldom attributed to the ways these systems shape our lives. The pain is felt and remembered; yet its source is displaced.

To that extent, debt in the relationship of ordinary users of credit cards, takers of loans, and holders of mortgages and insurance policies could be seen as a sort of buffered financial experience, in which we are taught to regularly forget the trauma of waiting, interruption, billing cycles, and credit decision delays. We are buffered subjects, whose buffering does not (as the dictionary meaning of the terms suggests) shield us from harm, but in fact habituates us to forget the memory of the last harm so as to be innocent and hopeful when we experience the next one. The result, as we proposed in chapter 2, is a planned obsolescence of technologies, bodies, and social structures.

In this book, we have paid more attention to the commonalities between Silicon Valley and Wall Street than the differences, because our aim was to focus on failure, not on a macro-understanding of everything that links digitality, innovation, and finance in the contemporary moment. Still, it is worth stating that there is a deep need to examine more closely the ways in which digital and financial capital differ, and also in which they connect, to create the complex operating system of contemporary capitalism. That is a task that is beyond the scope of this book, which provided a model of how the two cultures that have come to define our world could be studied together. We are thus convinced that the right approach to this larger problem is not to stress either similarities or differences between these two expressions of contemporary capitalism but to look at their links, overlaps, and mutually supportive affordances. This is sure to require a broad new approach to the relationships between risk, innovation, speculation, and digitality, as key elements of the architecture of the promise machine today, a matter that the theme of failure can initiate but not exhaust.

To resist the celebratory narrative promoted by both Silicon Valley and Wall Street, we must first learn to remember failure better. It is therefore not enough to recast failure as a subversive technique or to reappropriate it in order to resist the neoliberal binary of "failure" and "success". Embracing or "queering" failure, as joyful and liberating as this process can be, faces real challenges in an era of entrepreneurial spirit built on a beta culture of endless testing. When Silicon Valley CEOs and the *Harvard Business Review* urge employees to fail faster and better, any attempt to reclaim failure as a queer way out of the straightjacket of "toxic positivity" (Halberstam 2011) might backfire by buying into the ethos of creative destruction. In short, the attempt to make failure more disruptive needs to be once again re-examined in the age of "disruption."

Can failure still hold subversive meaning? While leaving this question open, we would like to chart a few possible pathways toward a meaningful resistance of its monetization. We should be more forceful in demanding accountability from companies, engineers, computer scientists, shareholders, and executives. We should press governmental agencies and legislatures to limit the use of ethically dubious business models like planned obsolescence and, instead, to promote legislation such as "the right to repair." We should strive to develop digital and algorithmic literacy that can help us to "un-blackbox" our opaque devices and to better understand the infrastructures they rely on. And, most importantly, we can promote a way of thinking that resists the horizon of endless choice and endorses a culture of repair, slow growth, and debt aversion. Finally, though we do not know how to craft new regulatory policies, we believe that regulators need to find ways to stay ahead of the world of both digital and financial innovation, to provide social precautions which precede new instruments, tools, and platforms before they collapse, implode, or vanish with our money and our time. This is a space for collaboration between state and civil society.

The promise machine reshapes the way we relate to our technologies, our environment, our loved ones, and our horizon of possibility. It serves to deny real catastrophe such as bankruptcy or climate change, recasting them as part of a myth of endless progress. These very real failures, when they come, will make a real difference in the lives of millions and, eventually, in the survival of the human species and the planet it inhabits. The answer is thus not to forgive and forget, or to reclaim failure as revolutionary; the answer is failure, remembered.

References

Ahmed, S. (2004). Affective economies. *Social Text*, 22, 117–39.

Ahmed, S. (2010). *The Promise of Happiness*. Durham, NC: Duke University Press.

Alexander, N. (2016). Catered to your future self: Netflix's predictive personalization and the quantification of taste. In K. McDonald and D. Smith-Rowsey (eds.), *The Netflix Effect: Technology and Entertainment in the Twenty-First Century*. New York: Bloomsbury Academic, pp. 81–98.

Alexander, N. (2017). Rage against the machine: Buffering, noise, and perpetual anxiety in the age of connected viewing. *Cinema Journal*, 56, 1–24.

Alexander, N. (2019). *Chronopower: On-Demand Culture and Its Disconnects*. PhD thesis. New York University.

Ammori, M. (2014). The case for net neutrality. *Foreign Affairs*, January, 62–3.

References

Anderson, M. (2017). Digital divide persists even as lower-income Americans make gains in tech adoption. *Pew Research Center.* Available at: https://www.pewresearch.org/fact-tank/2017/03/22/digital-divide-persists-even-as-lower-income-americans-ma ke-gains-in-tech-adoption/

Ante, S.E. (2008). *Creative Capital: Georges Doriot and the Birth of Venture Capital.* Boston, MA: Harvard Business Review Press.

Appadurai, A. (2015). *Banking on Words: The Failure of Language in the Age of Derivative Finance.* Chicago, IL: University of Chicago Press.

Appadurai, A. (2016). Introduction to special issue of *Social Research* on failure, *Social Research,* 83 (3).

Appadurai, A. (2019). The scarcity of social futures in the digital era. In J. Andersson and S. Kemp (eds.), *Futures.* Oxford: Oxford University Press.

Austin, J.L. (1975). *How to Do Things with Words.* Cambridge, MA: Harvard University Press.

Ayache, E. (2010). *The Blank Swan: The End of Probability.* Chichester: John Wiley & Sons.

Baker, P., Hanson, J., and Hunsinger, J. (eds.) (2013). *The Unconnected: Social Justice, Participation, and Engagement in the Information Society.* New York: Peter Lang.

Bao, Y., Berkowitz, D., and Wren, B.M. (2010). Consumer marketing of high-technology products. In H. Bidgoli (ed.), *The Handbook of Technology Management, Supply Chain Management, Marketing and Advertising, and Global Management, Vol.* 2. Hoboken, NJ: John Wiley & Sons, pp. 290–304.

References

Barker, T. (2018). *Against Transmission: Media Philosophy and the Engineering of Time*. New York: Bloomsbury Academic.

Bateson, G. (1972). *Steps to an Ecology of Mind*. New York: Chandler Publishing Co.

Beck, U. (1986). *Risk Society: Towards a New Modernity*. London: Sage Publications.

Beckert, J. (2016). *Imagined Futures: Fictional Expectations and Capitalist Dynamics*. Cambridge, MA: Harvard University Press.

Beckett, S. (1995). *Nohow On: Company, Ill Seen Ill Said, Worstward Ho: Three Novels*. New York: Grove Press.

Belton, J. (2009). The story of 50mm film. *The Velvet Light Trap*, 64, 84–5.

Berlant, L. (2010). Risky bigness: On obesity, eating, and the ambiguity of "health." In J.M. Metzl and A. Kirkland (eds.), *Against Health: How Health Became the New Morality*. New York: NYU Press, pp. 26–39.

Berlant, L. (2011). *Cruel Optimism*. Durham, NC: Duke University Press.

Bogost, I. (2017). Network neutrality can't fix the internet. *The Atlantic*, November 22. Available at: https://www.theatlantic.com/technology/archive/2017/11/network-neutrality-cant-fix-the-internet/546620

Bordwell, D. (1985). *Narration in the Fiction Film*. Madison, WI: University of Wisconsin Press.

Bourdieu, P. (1977). *Outline of a Theory of Practice*. Cambridge: Cambridge University Press.

Bower, J.L. and Christensen, C. (1995). Disruptive technologies: Catching the wave. *Harvard Business Review*, 7 (1), 43–53.

References

Brown, W. (1995). *States of Injury: Power and Freedom in Late Modernity*. Princeton, NJ: Princeton University Press.

Brunton, F. and Nissenbaum, H. (2015). *Obfuscation: A User's Guide for Privacy and Protest*. Cambridge, MA: The MIT Press.

Burke, J.G. (1966). Bursting boilers and the Federal power. *Technology and Culture*, 7 (1), 1–23.

Campolo, A., Sanfilippo, M., Whittaker, M., and Crawford, K. (2017). *The AI Now 2017 Report*. New York: The AI Now Institute.

CBS News (2018). 5G service is coming – and so are health concerns over the towers that support it. Available at: https://www.cbsnews.com/news/5g-network-cell-towers-raise-health-concerns-for-some-residents/

Cheney-Lippold, J. (2017). *We Are Data: Algorithms and the Making of Our Digital Selves*. New York: NYU Press.

Chu, B. (2018). Global debt: Why has it hit an all-time high? And how worried should we be about it? *The Independent*. Available at: https://www.independent.co.uk/news/business/analysis-and-features/global-debt-crisis-explained-all-time-high-world-economy-causes-solutions-definition-a8143516.html

Chun, W.H.K. (2008). On "sourcery," or code as fetish. *Configurations*, 16, 299–324.

Chun, W.H.K. (2016). *Updating to Remain the Same: Habitual New Media*. Cambridge, MA: The MIT Press.

Cubitt, S. (2011). Current screens. In O. Grau and T. Veigl (eds.), *Imagery in the Twenty-First Century*. Cambridge, MA: The MIT Press, pp. 21–35.

Cubitt, S. (2014). *The Practice of Light: A Genealogy of*

Visual Technologies from Prints to Pixels. Cambridge, MA: The MIT Press.

Cvetkovich, A. (2012). *Depression: A Public Feeling*. Durham, NC: Duke University Press.

Daub, A. (2018). The undertakers of Silicon Valley. *Logic Magazine*, 5, 19–31.

Easterling, K. (2016). Histories of things that don't happen and shouldn't always work. *Social Research*, 83 (3), 625–44.

Evans, B. (2016). In praise of failure. *Ben-evans.com*. Available at: https://www.ben-evans.com/benedict-evans/2016/4/28/winning-and-losing

Farman, J. (2017). How buffer icons shape our sense of time and our practices of waiting. [Blog] *Delayed Response*. Available at: http://jasonfarman.com/del ayedresponse/loading-how-buffer-icons-shape-our-sense-of-time-and-our-practices-of-waiting/

Farman, J. (2018). *Delayed Response: The Art of Waiting from the Ancient to the Instant World*. New Haven, CT: Yale University Press.

Fried, C. (1981). *Contract as Promise: A Theory of Contractual Obligation*. Cambridge, MA: Harvard University Press.

Galloway, R.A. (2004). *Protocol: How Control Exists After Decentralization*. Cambridge, MA: The MIT Press.

Gartenberg, C. (2018). The US government is investigating Apple over slowed-down iPhones. *The Verge*. Available at: https://www.theverge.com/2018/1/30/16951328/ apple-iphone-battery-slow-down-software-update-de partment-of-justice-sec-investigation-probe

Ginsburg, F. (2008). Rethinking the Digital Age. In D. Hesmondhalgh and J. Toynbee (eds.), *The Media*

References

and Social Theory. New York: Routledge, pp. 127–44.

Goffman, E. (1974). *Frame Analysis: An Essay on the Organization of Experience*. Boston, MA: Northeastern University Press.

Goldberg, G. (2018). *Antisocial Media: Anxious Labor in the Digital Economy*. New York: NYU Press.

Graeber, D. (2011). *Debt: The First 5,000 Years*. New York: Melville House.

Graham, S. and Thrift, N. (2007). Out of order: Understanding repair and maintenance. *Theory, Culture & Society*, 24, 1–25.

Grosz, E. (2013). Habit today: Ravaisson, Bergson, Deleuze and Us. *Body & Society*, 19 (2–3), 217–39.

Halberstam, J. (2011). *The Queer Art of Failure*. Durham, NC: Duke University Press.

Hasbrouck, J. and Saar, G. (2013). Low-latency trading. *Journal of Financial Markets*, 16 (4), 646–79.

Hass, N. (2013). And the award for the next HBO goes to … *GQ*. Available at: https://www.gq.com/story/netflix-founder-reed-hastings-house-of-cards-arrested-development

Heller, N. (2017). Is the gig economy working? *The New Yorker*. Available at: https://www.newyorker.com/magazine/2017/05/15/is-the-gig-economy-working

Hilderbrand, L. (2009). *Inherent Vice: Bootleg Histories of Videotape and Copyright*. Durham, NC: Duke University Press.

Hoefle, M. (2012). Joseph A. Schumpeter – Preceptor of change. *Managerism*, Lesson No. 39. Available at: https://www.managerism.org/topics/relectures/lesson-no-39

References

Holt, J. and Sanson, K. (eds.) (2013). *Connected Viewing: Selling, Streaming, and Sharing Media in the Digital Age*. New York: Routledge.

Hooda, S. (2017). Every Jeff Bezos' Letter to Shareholders since 1997. *Medium*, April 13. Available at: https://medium.com/@hooda/every-jeff-bezos-letter-to-share holders-since-1997-b3cb57914cab

Horning, R. (2014). "Sharing" economy and self-exploitation. *The New Inquiry*. Available at: https://thenewinquiry.com/blog/sharing-economy-and-self-exploitation

Hu, T. (2016). *A Prehistory of the Cloud*. Cambridge, MA: The MIT Press.

Jacobs, J. (2011). Television, interrupted: Pollution or aesthetic? In J. Bennett and N. Strange (eds.), *Television as Digital Media*. Durham, NC: Duke University Press, pp. 255–81.

Janeja, A. and Bandak, A. (eds.) (2018). *Ethnographies of Waiting*. New York: Bloomsbury Publishing.

Janeway W.H. (2012). *Doing Capitalism in the Innovation Economy: Reconfiguring the Three-Player Game between Markets, Speculators and the State*. Cambridge: Cambridge University Press.

Jarzombek, M. (2016). *Digital Stockholm Syndrome in the Post-ontological Age*. Minneapolis, MN: University of Minnesota Press.

Jenkins, H. (2006). *Convergence Culture: Where Old and New Media Collide*. New York: NYU Press.

Jervis, F. (Forthcoming). *Eating the World: The Political Economy of Silicon Valley*. PhD thesis. New York University.

Jones, M. (2016). Why this market rally looks like a classic investor trap. *MarketWatch*. Available at: https://

References

www.marketwatch.com/story/why-this-market-rally-looks-like-a-classic-investor-trap-2016-04-14

Kahneman, D. and Riis, J. (2005). Living, and thinking about it: Two perspectives on life. In F.A. Huppert, N. Baylis, and B. Keverne (eds.), *The Science of Well-Being*. Oxford: Oxford University Press, pp. 285–304.

Keough, D.R. (2011). *The Ten Commandments for Business Failure*. New York: Portfolio/Penguin.

Kessler, S. (2018). *Gigged: The End of the Job and the Future of Work*. New York: St. Martin's Press.

Knight, F. (1921). *Risk, Uncertainty and Profit*. Boston, MA: Houghton Mifflin.

Koebler, J. (2017). Apple's iPhone throttling will reinvigorate the push for right to repair laws. *Motherboard*. Available at: https://motherboard.vice.com/en_us/article/a3nvmk/apple-iphone-throttling-right-to-repair

Lazzarato, M. (2012). *The Making of the Indebted Man: An Essay on the Neoliberal Condition*. Cambridge, MA: The MIT Press.

Leahy, S. (2017). Each U.S. family trashes 400 iPhones' worth of e-waste a year. *National Geographic News*. Available at: https://news.nationalgeographic.com/2017/12/e-waste-monitor-report-glut/

Lin, L.Y., et al. (2016). Association between social media use and depression among U.S. young adults. *Depression and Anxiety*, 33, 323–31.

Manovich, L. (2002). *The Language of New Media*. Cambridge, MA: The MIT Press.

Mantz, J.W. (2008). Improvisational economies: Coltan production in the Eastern Congo. *Social Anthropology*, 16, 34–50.

Marx, K. (1887). *Capital*. Moscow: Progress Publishers.

Mattern, S. (2019). Data fantasies and operational facts: Infrastructural epistemologies. *Society of Cinema and Media Studies Annual Conference*, Seattle, March.

Maxwell, J.C. (2000). *Failing Forward: Turning Mistakes into Stepping Stones for Success*. Nashville, TN: Thomas Nelson.

Maxwell, R. and Miller, T. (2012). *Greening the Media*. New York: Oxford University Press.

Mazzucato, M. (2016). *The Value of Everything: Making and Taking in the Global Economy*. New York: Public Affairs.

Möhlmann, M. and Zalmanson, L. (2017). Hands on the wheel: Navigating algorithmic management and Uber drivers' autonomy. *International Conference on Information Systems*, Seoul, South Korea.

Morozov, E. (2013). *To Save Everything, Click Here: The Folly of Technological Solutionism*. New York: Public Affairs.

Mozur, P. (2018). A genocide incited on Facebook, with posts from Myanmar's military. *The New York Times*, October 15. Available at: https://www.nytimes.com/2018/10/15/technology/myanmar-facebook-genocide.html

Nakamura, L. (2009). Plug and play: Performances of risk and failure in digital media presentations. *The Velvet Light Trap*, 64, 87–9.

Nielsen, J. (2018) Nielsen's Law of Internet Bandwidth. Available at: https://www.nngroup.com/articles/law-of-bandwidth/

O'Neil, C. (2016). *Weapons of Math Destruction: How Big Data Increases Inequality and Threatens Democracy*. New York: Broadway Books.

Packard, V. (1960). *The Waste Makers*. Philadelphia, PA: David McKay Co.

Pariser, E. (2012). *The Filter Bubble: How the New Personalized Web Is Changing What We Read and How We Think*. New York: Penguin Books.

Parks, L. and Starosielski, N. (eds.) (2015). *Signal Traffic: Critical Studies of Media Infrastructures*. Champaign, IL: University of Illinois Press.

Pasquale, F. (2016). *The Black Box Society: The Secret Algorithms that Control Money and Information*. Cambridge, MA: Harvard University Press.

Petruska, K. and Vanderhoef, J. (2014). TV that watches you: Data collection and the connected living room. *Spectator*, 34 (2).

Plantin, J.C. and Punathambekar, A. (2019). Digital media infrastructures: Pipes, platforms, and politics. *Media, Culture & Society*, 41 (2), 163–74.

Popper, K. (1963). *Conjectures and Refutations: The Growth of Scientific Knowledge*. London: Routledge.

Proctor, R.N. and Schiebinger, L. (eds.) (2008). *Agnotology: The Making and Unmaking of Ignorance*. Stanford, CA: Stanford University Press.

Raphael, R. (2017). Netflix CEO Reed Hastings: Sleep is our competition. *Fast Company*. Available at: https://www.fastcompany.com/40491939/netflix-ceo-reed-hastings-sleep-is-our-competition

Rose, N. (1999). *Powers of Freedom: Reframing Political Thought*. Cambridge: Cambridge University Press.

Rosenblat, A. (2018a). *Uberland: How Algorithms Are Rewriting the Rules of Work*. Oakland, CA: University of California Press.

Rosenblat, A. (2018b). When your boss is an algorithm. *The New York Times*, October 12. Available at: https://www.nytimes.com/2018/10/12/opinion/sund ay/uber-driver-life.html

Russell, A.L. and Vinsel, L. (2018). After innovation, turn to maintenance. *Technology and Culture*, 59 (1), 1–25.

Russell, C. (2018). 5G wireless telecommunications expansion: Public health and environmental implications. *Environmental Research*, 165, 484–95.

Sanger, D.E., Barnes, J.E., Zhong, R., and Santora, M. (2019). In 5G race with China, U.S. pushes allies to fight Huawei. *The New York Times*, January 26. Available at: https://www.nytimes.com/2019/01/26/us/politics/huawei-china-us-5g-technology.html

Saval, N. (2019). Uber and the ongoing erasure of public life. *The New Yorker*, February 18. Available at: https://www.newyorker.com/culture/dept-of-design/uber-and-the-ongoing-erasure-of-public-life

Schüll, N.D. (2014). *Addiction by Design: Machine Gambling in Las Vegas*. Princeton, NJ: Princeton University Press.

Schumpeter, J. (1942). *Capitalism, Socialism and Democracy*. Floyd, VA: Impact Books.

Scudamore, B. and Williams, R. (2018). *WTF?! (Willing to Fail): How Failure Can Be Your Key to Success*. Austin, TX: Lioncrest Publishing.

Shabi, R. (2002). The e-waste land. *Guardian Weekend*, November 30, 36–43.

Shannon, C.E. and Weaver, W. (1975). *The Mathematical Theory of Communication*. Urbana, IL: University of Illinois Press.

Slade, G. (2007). *Made to Break: Technology and*

References

Obsolescence in America. Cambridge, MA: Harvard University Press.

Smith, J.T. (2008). DVD technologies and the art of control. In J. Bennett and T. Brown (eds.), *Film and Television after DVD*. New York: Routledge, pp. 129–48.

Star, S.L. (1999). The ethnography of infrastructure. *American Behavioral Scientist*, 43 (3), 377–91.

Stark, L. and Rosenblat, A. (2016). Algorithmic labor and information asymmetries: A case study of Uber's drivers. *International Journal of Communication*, 10, 3758–84.

Starosielski, N. (2015). *The Undersea Network*. Durham, NC: Duke University Press.

Stephens, R. and Mahesh, A. (2018). *State of the App Economy*, 6th edn. Washington, DC: ACT/The App Association. Available at: https://actonline.org/wp-content/uploads/ACT_2018-State-of-the-App-Economy-Report_4.pdf

Sterne, J. (2009). The cat telephone. *The Velvet Light Trap*, 64, 83–4.

Sterne, J. (2012). *MP3: The Meaning of a Format*. Durham, NC: Duke University Press.

Steyerl, H. (2009). In defense of the poor image. *e-flux journal*. Available at: http://www.e-flux.com/journal/in-defense-of-the-poor-image/

Steyerl, H. (2014). Proxy politics: Signal and noise. *e-flux journal*. Available at:. https://www.e-flux.com/journal/60/61045/proxy-politics-signal-and-noise/

Tawil-Souri, H. (2017). Checkpoint time. *Qui Parle: Critical Humanities and Social Sciences*, 26 (2), 383–422.

Terranova, T. (2000). Free labor: Producing

culture for the digital economy. *Social Text*, 18, 33–58.

Tett, G. (2010) Silos and silences: Why so few people spotted the problems in complex credit and what that implies for the future. *Financial Stability Review*, 14, 121–9.

Thackara, J. (2005). *In the Bubble: Designing in a Complex World*. Cambridge, MA: The MIT Press.

Tierney, T.F. (1993). *The Value of Convenience: A Genealogy of Technical Culture*. Albany, NY: SUNY Press.

Tonkinwise, C. (2016). Failing to sense the future: From design to the proactionary test drive. *Social Research*, 83 (3), 597–624.

Veblen, T. (1898). Why is economics not an evolutionary science? *Quarterly Journal of Economics*, 12 (3), 373–97.

Verbeek, P. (2004). *What Things Do: Philosophical Reflections on Technology, Agency and Design*. University Park, PA: Penn State University Press.

Wiener, N. (1965). *Cybernetics, Or Control and Communication in the Animal and the Machine*. Cambridge, MA: The MIT Press.

Wosnitzer, R. (2014). *Desk, Firm, God, Country: Proprietary Trading and the Speculative Ethos of Financialism*. PhD thesis, New York University.

Index

5G networks 85–6, 87
affective economy 7, 10, 11, 25,
    31–5, 75
  based on anxiety, helplessness
    and constant denial 93
  failure functions as 92
  planned obsolescence 41
Ahmed, Sara 6, 7, 11, 25, 31–2,
    33, 35, 92
AI (artificial intelligence) 28, 65,
    67, 77
Alexander, Neta 57, 72, 92
algorithmic identities 62,
    63
algorithmic systems 29, 58, 63,
    65, 119
  biased 75
algorithms 33, 34, 57, 61,
    64, 66, 67, 68, 78, 81,
    124
  machine-learning 28, 120
Amazon 4, 51, 60–1, 77–8, 80,
    81, 84
Appadurai, Arjun 14, 36, 37,
    61, 96, 98, 103

Apple 27, 51, 76, 84
  iPhone 24, 83
  Lisa computer 23
ARDC (American Research and
    Development Corporation)
    52
Austin, J. L. 21, 37, 38, 39, 98,
    99, 102, 103, 106

bailouts 113
Baker, P. 58–9, 74
bankruptcies 96, 110, 115, 116,
    125
banks 10, 21,14, 15, 17, 110,
    112, 113, 115, 116, 118
  distinction between venture
    capitalists and 40, 41
  see also big banks; investment
    banks
behavioral theory 91
Berlant, Lauren 6, 44–5
Bezos, Jeff 77–8
big banks 112, 113, 114
black boxes 8, 13–14, 29, 33,
    34, 66, 69, 96, 115, 124

Index

Blockbuster (video rental) 36
buffering 9, 13, 18, 20, 41,
    69–71 73, 75, 80, 81, 88,
    90–2, 93, 95, 106, 108,
    117, 123
  habitual new media and
    87–92
  ignored 75, 88
  perpetual anxiety induced by
    18, 32, 92
business cycle 35, 36

California 24, 83
  see also LA; Silicon Valley
capitalism 3, 6, 9, 11, 25, 36,
    48, 50, 61, 65, 108, 112,
    113, 116
  calculating attitude of 35
  digital 11, 16
  failure an inherent feature of
    35, 36
  financialized 68, 97, 111, 121
  information 33, 76
  prediction of collapse 36, 49
  self-destruction of 51
  speculative 39–40
  see also contemporary
    capitalism; industrial
    capitalism; VCs
Cheney-Lippold, John 34, 61,
    62–3
China 87
Chun, Wendy H. K. 17, 23, 76,
    87–8, 89
CinemaScope 22
commodity markets 100
connectivity 22, 34, 54, 58, 68
  constant WiFi 42
  convenience and 59, 60, 61,
    68
  seamless 16, 42
consumer debt 10, 15, 111,
    113, 114, 116
contemporary capitalism 2, 11,
    68, 120, 122, 123,

convenience 14, 21, 45, 48, 49,
    52, 57, 59–63, 65–6, 68
  see also promise of
    convenience
creative destruction 5, 36,
    46–69, 120, 124
credit 11, 25, 44, 61, 87, 99,
    109, 116
  bank-generated 113
  decision delays 96, 123
  risk-based trading 105
  waiting for approvals 13,
    105
credit cards 96, 113, 122
cruel optimism see toxic
    positivity
Cubitt, Sean 24, 76

Darwin, Charles 56
debt 10, 11, 15, 17, 21, 25, 37,
    39, 40–1, 44, 62, 69, 87,
    95–8, 105, 107, 111–14,
    121–2, 124
  cycle of 17
  endless producers of 16
  global 113
  habitual 112
  market failure and 108–15
  monetization of 112, 121
  reliance on 96
  student 109, 118
  see also consumer debt
debt production 95, 108, 110,
    116, 120–1
delayed promises 21, 39–40,
    55
  of seamlessness 41, 71, 92,
    93–4
denial of failure 21–5, 49, 66–7
derivatives 11, 14–16, 20,
    24, 25, 36–7, 39, 41, 94,
    97–108, 110, 114, 122
  logic of 14, 109
  rise of 3
  toxic 104

Index

derivatives market
  analysis of corrosive
    workings of 62
  collapse of failed promises
    represented by 115
  global, direct link between
    consumer debt and
    113
  success of 116
digital networks 3, 72
divisions of labor 28
DVDs (digital video/versatile
    disks) 72, 120

economy of failure 7, 35–7
  affective 31–5
  political 25
EFSF (European Financial
    Stability Facility) 113

Facebook 51, 53, 60, 83, 84
  see also Zuckerberg
failed promises 11, 16, 41, 42,
    99
  accumulation and scale of
    97
  collapse of 115
  re-established 112–13
  systemic and risky 37
Farman, J. 14, 81, 82, 83
Federal Communications
    Commission (US) 85
felicity conditions 38, 97, 98,
    101, 103, 106–7
financialization 6, 66, 68, 97,
    99, 111
futures markets 100, 106

Galloway, Alexander 88–9
GIF (graphics interchange
    format) 71, 72, 79, 88,
    89, 90
gig economy 3, 12, 45, 47, 53,
    55–6
  backlash against 54

exploitation and information
    asymmetry 63
  proliferation of 43, 48
Ginsburg, Faye 13, 74
Goldberg, Greg 53, 56, 67
Google 51, 81
Google Assistant 52, 83–4
Google AutoComplete 75
Graham, S. 7, 8, 25, 27, 28–9
gratification 106
  see also instant gratification
Great Recession (2007–9) 10,
    14, 41
Grosz, Elizabeth 89, 90

habitual failure 9, 15–19, 69,
    93–5, 118, 120, 122
  buffering is an example of 95
  consumer debt and 116
Halberstam, Jack 6, 7, 124
happiness 42, 71, 91, 96, 110
  neoliberal promise of 6
Harvard Business Review 124
Harvard Business School 51–2
Hastings, Reed 73, 78
hedge funds 14, 17
  aggressively pushing into new
    markets 110
  competitive advantage 81
  mega-profits streamed
    upwards to 15
  obscene profits 113
Heidegger, Martin 25, 26, 27,
    32
HFT (high-frequency trading)
    81
housing mortgages 99, 113
  subprime 103
Hu Tung-Hui 21–2
Huawei 87
Hulu 80

identity 57, 59–63, 68
  algorithmic 62, 63
  collective 47

Index

immateriality 16
  digital 22, 78
  myth of 76–80, 94
  supposed 28
immediacy 73
  convenience and 21, 48
  understanding of 72
  utopian network offering 75
industrial capitalism
  competition among firms in 56
  logic of 50
  Marx's central insight about the workings of 110–11
  primary dynamic force of 47
information asymmetry 29, 33, 63, 94, 115
innovation 4–5, 7, 9, 12, 15, 35–6, 40, 52, 56, 58, 67–8, 98–9, 123–4
  design 54
  entrepreneurial 50
  financial 10, 124
  idea that failure is key to 10
  monetization of 10
  obsolescence and 116
  risk, failure, futurity and 46
  Schumpeter on 5, 48–51
  see also technological innovation
Instagram 53, 58
instant gratification 14, 21, 42, 66
insurance 44, 99–100, 104, 109–10, 113, 114
  health 55
  inadequate coverage 17
  medical 121
insurance policies 17, 96, 122
  unaffordable 115
intellectual property 29, 76
internet 22, 59, 63, 71–2, 73, 81
  access to 74, 92, 93
  control of 84

ever-growing dependency on connectivity 93
  the future of 85
  high-speed 75, 80
  immune to failure 21
  slow 82
  smartphone-only users 83
  see also GIF; IoT; ISPs
investment banks 14
IoT (Internet of Things) 33, 52, 85
IPOs (initial public offerings) 6, 77
ISPs (internet service providers) 44, 70

Knight, Frank 5, 15

language 1, 16, 48, 66, 67, 98
  corporate leadership 77
  failure of 98
  link between derivatives and 102
latency 16, 70, 71, 75, 77
  false 3, 13, 80–7
  monetization of 108
Lyft 54, 65, 68

market failure 36–7, 116
  classic example of 96
  debt and 108–15
  techno-failure and 20–45, 105, 119
Marvel Studios 82
Marx, Karl 35, 36, 49, 76, 109, 110–11
  M-C-M formula 105
materiality 26
  see also immateriality
Mattern, Shannon 74, 86
memory 59, 123
  buffering connected to cognitive function of 91
  collective 2, 23
  digital 88

Index

failure of 13
role in judgment of failure 70
selective 88
visual 23
Microsoft 24, 51
monetization 103, 105
debt 112, 121
digital services 80
environmental 109
forgetfulness and ignorance 3
innovation: financial 10;
technological 10
mortgage 109
risk 109, 111; financial 97
uncertainty 33–4
monetization of failure 10, 13,
19, 21, 35, 57, 69
analysis of buffering can
reveal 80
meaningful resistance of 124
reliance on 121
technological 70
monetization of waiting 3, 70,
79, 108
buffering and 13
detailed argument about 69
false latency and 6, 13, 80–7
Moore's Law 73, 78
mortgages 17, 96, 103–5, 109,
112, 114–16, 121–2
key to the 2007–8 crisis 97
see also housing mortgages

Nakamura, Lisa 22, 25, 94
Netflix 36, 43, 73, 78, 80, 84,
119, 120
Comcast deal (2015) 75
official technology blog 76–7
New York 81, 120
see also Wall Street
New York Times, The 53

obsolescence 48, 55, 69
induced 46
innovation and 116

psychological, progressive, or
dynamic 31
social structures 13, 31, 70
see also planned obsolescence
opting out 119–20
fantasy of 68–9

partners/employees 63–8
Pasquale, Frank 29, 61
pension funds 17, 115
performatives 37, 38, 39, 98,
99, 101, 102
chain of 103, 107, 116
planned obsolescence 8, 23–4,
30, 41, 123–4
Popper, Karl 3–4, 25
PowerPoint 22–3
promise of convenience 11,
42–5, 46, 122
fulfilling 78
proliferation of mobile apps
and 48
prominent 21
promises
agonistic 21, 38–9, 106,
107
Austinian 21, 37, 39, 98;
pure 38, 106
broken 11, 21, 37–41
contractual 103
derivative 102–8
neoliberal 6, 92
performative 38
unfulfilled 41
see also delayed promises;
failed promises; promise of
convenience

queer studies 3, 6–7, 25

Reddit 58
risk-taking 12, 15, 17, 36, 109
digital 16
irresponsible 98
speculative 108

143

Index

Rosenblat, Alex 53–4, 56, 64–5, 66, 67
Russell, Andrew L. 7–8, 9, 86

Samsung 24, 27
Saval, Nikil 63–4
Schumpeter, J. A. 5, 12, 35–6, 47–59, 67
Seamless (mobile app) 43
seamlessness 16, 42, 57, 74, 80, 89, 91, 96
  infinite 28
  promise of 90; delayed 41, 70–1, 92, 93–4
Shannon, Claude 71
Silicon Valley 3, 6, 9, 24, 37, 77, 92, 106, 107
  bedrock of 15
  broken promise perpetuated by 21
  giants of 36, 51, 52, 82
  key to speculative risk-taking 108
  latency used to maximize profit 82
  logic and business model of 71
  mammoth investments in promising startups 105
  most important players in 15
  perennial beta-tester of 116
  promise of seamlessness and limitless access to information made by 41
  Schumpeter in 5, 12, 36, 51–9
  world of 14; speculative 48
  see also Silicon Valley and failure; Wall Street and Silicon Valley
Silicon Valley and failure 20–1, 124
  attitude toward 10
  centrality and strategic use of 25

ethos of 4
monetization of 35
remembered or ignored 118
tolerance for 40
smartphones 24, 26, 42, 53, 120
social blankness 29
social media see Facebook; Instagram; Reddit; Twitter; WhatsApp
social structures 123
  long-lasting 48
  obsolescence of 13, 31; rapid 70
  understanding of 63
sociality 13, 15, 46–69
Sony 76
Spotify 57
Stark, Luke 64–5
Starosielski, Nicole 22, 72
Steyerl, Hito 61, 79

TARP (US Troubled Asset Relief Program) 113
TaskRabbit 53, 58
Tawil-Souri, Helga 14, 74, 106
techno-failure 11–12, 71, 72, 116
  epistemology of 25–31
  market failure and 20–45, 105, 119
  monetized 70
  two-fold process of 17–18
  understanding of 84
technological innovation 11, 44, 78, 82
  blind faith in 4
  described as key driver of profit and wealth 56
  Silicon Valley monetizes 10
Thrift, N. 7, 8, 25, 27, 28–9
Tierney, Thomas 21, 42–3, 66, 93
Tinder 57, 58
TOD (time-on-device) 57

Index

toxic positivity 6, 7, 124
Trump, Donald 85, 87

Uber 43, 47, 53–5, 58, 63–8
United States 28, 30, 36, 108
  financial system failure
    (2007–8) 98
  mortgage market of recent
    years 104
  obesity epidemic 44
  see also California; Chicago;
    Federal Communications
    Commission; Florida; New
    York; TARP; Trump

VCs (venture capitalists) 10,
  12–13, 15, 39, 51–2, 63
  distinction between bankers
    and 40, 41
  see also Andreessen
    Horowitz; ARDC; HBP
Veblen, Thorstein 56
Verizon 82, 86
Vinsel, Lee 7–8, 9

waiting 13–14, 24, 34, 73
  anxiety and 106
  built-in 83
  commodification of 82–3
  economy of 105
  important role in production
    of intimacy and attachment
    93

liminality of 75
  meanings of 74
  phenomenological mode of
    90
  trauma of 96, 122
  viewing as 32
  see also buffering;
    monetization of waiting
Wall Street 3, 10, 14–15, 21,
  37, 51, 82, 105, 106, 107,
  115
  promises made by 41, 108
  reliance on debt produced
    and exploited by 96
  system of denial in 18
Wall Street and failure 9–10,
  15, 20–1, 25, 108, 118
Wall Street and Silicon Valley
  commonalities between 123
  differences between 10
  effort to connect 96
  oil that connects 122
  symbiosis between 11
Weber, Max 5, 35, 49
WhatsApp 53
WiFi (wireless networking
  technology) 53, 60
  constant connectivity 42
  growing dependency on 81
  hotspots 80
Wix Turbo 82

Zuckerberg, Mark 23

145